THE LAKE DISTRICT

A CENTURY OF CONSERVATION

GEOFFREY BERRY AND GEOFFREY BEARD

The Lake District
A Century of Conservation

JOHN BARTHOLOMEW & SON LIMITED

EDINBURGH

First published in Great Britain 1980 by
JOHN BARTHOLOMEW & SON LIMITED
12 Duncan Street, Edinburgh EH9 1TA

ISBN 0 7028 8290 9

Book and jacket design: Douglas Martin Associates, Leicester
Set in Palatino, 10/13 pt, 9/10½ pt

British Library Cataloguing in Publication Data
Berry, Geoffrey
The Lake District: A Century of Conservation
1. Lake District, Eng. – Economic conditions
2. Man – Influence on nature – England
– Lake District
I. Title   II. Beard, Geoffrey
330.9′427′8081   HC257.L32

Reproduced, printed and bound in Great Britain by
Hazell Watson & Viney Ltd, Aylesbury, Bucks

Is then no nook of English ground secure
From rash assault? Schemes of retirement sown
In youth, and 'mid the busy world kept pure
As when their earliest flowers of hope were blown,
Must perish; – how can they this blight endure?
And must he too the ruthless change bemoan
Who scorns a false utilitarian lure
'Mid his paternal fields at random thrown?
Baffle the threat, bright scene, from Orrest-head
Given to the pausing traveller's rapturous glance:
Plead for thy peace, thou beautiful romance
Of nature: and, if human hearts be dead,
Speak, passing winds; ye torrents, with your strong
And constant voice, protest against the wrong.

William Wordsworth
Sonnet on the Projected Kendal and Windermere Railway 1844

Contents

Preface   xi

PART ONE

I	Early Years of 'Rash Assault'	1
II	The Water of Mammon	6
III	The Coniferous Mass	13
IV	High and Low Roads	21
V	The Carriage Trade	35
VI	Light to Work By	42
VII	Conclusion	53

Notes to Part One   55

PART TWO

1   Thirlmere: the dam
2   Thirlmere: afforestation
3   Crummock Water: water abstraction
4   Haweswater: extent of draw-down
5   Haweswater: effects of draw-down
6   Haweswater: access in the valley
7   Mardale Church, c.1920: victim of Haweswater scheme
8   Bassenthwaite Lake: control proposals
9   Swindale: once threatened valley
10   Ullswater: abstraction with minimal draw-down
11   Ullswater: what future?
12   Longsleddale: survived railway scheme
13   Ennerdale: successive proposals for water abstraction
14   Ennerdale: normal level
15   Ennerdale: drawn-down
16   Newby Bridge: strategic point in abstraction and road schemes
17   Oxendale Beck: flood prevention work
18   Wet Sleddale Footbridge: flood threat
19   Wet Sleddale Footbridge: saved and reconstructed
20   Stott Park Bobbin Mill, Finsthwaite: symbol of a dying industry
21   Ennerdale: afforestation
22   Pillar Mountain: regimented spruce
23   Pillar Mountain: commands the dale

24   Duddon Valley: setting limits to afforestation
25   Upper Eskdale: saved from afforestation
26   Gill Bank above Boot in Eskdale: a way of life preserved
27   Borrowdale: broadleaved woodland saved
28   Bowness-on-Windermere: example of tree-planting
29   Rusland Beeches: trees preserved
30   Martindale: casualty of war recovered
31   Thirlmere: securing access to the valley
32   Hardknott Pass: the need for traffic management
33   A591 at Lowwood: the threat of 'improvement'
34   Wrynose Pass: example of traffic congestion
35   A591 Dunmail Raise: before reconstruction
36   A591 Dunmail Raise: after reconstruction
37   White Moss Common: successful management
38   A591 at Shoulthwaite: scale of roadworks
39   A591 by Windermere: commercial vehicles in the Lake District
40   Kirkstone Pass: heavy pressure on a narrow road
41   St John's Vale: setting for part of the reconstructed A66
42   Bridging the Greta Gorge in 1974: permanent domination
43   Bassenthwaite Lake: encroachment by a dual carriageway
44   A66 between Derwent Water and Bassenthwaite:
        striding across the valley
45   Protest on Latrigg: strength of concern for conservation
46   A66 across lower slopes of Latrigg: expensive and damaging
47   A66 near Keswick: unspoilt beauty
48   A66 near Keswick: imposition of an interchange
49   Kent Estuary: outstanding natural beauty preserved
50   Lindale bypass: on a grandiose scale
51   Borrowbeck Viaduct on M6: problem of routing a major highway
52   M6 in Lune Gorge: reasons for this route
53   Longsleddale: threat after threat
54   Levens Park: trees before cars?
55   Ambleside: at what cost a bypass?
56   Staveley: on what scale a bypass?
57   Great Gable: 1930s and '40s, the Lake District to be protected?
58   Upper Eskdale: 1948, F.L.D.'s fears and responses
59   Derwent Water: few visitors in winter
60   Great Langdale: conserving the commons
61   Stickle Tarn: the pattern of access in a National Park
62   Scafell: 'charter for the open air'
63   Near Patterdale: growth of the Upland Management Service
64   The Band: problem of eroded footpaths
65   Castle Crag: protecting access on foot
66   Brothers Water: preserving peace and tranquillity
67   'Kirby Quay' Coniston: restoring solitude and quietness
68   Limefitt Camp and Caravan Site: the cost of commercial
        development for tourism

69   Grasmere: venue for caravan rallies
70   On the southern boundary of the Lake District:
         controlling the impact of caravans
71   Finsthwaite: siting and screening car parks
72   Glencoyne Bay: hotels on wheels, the unacceptable face of tourism
73   Near Brothers Water: controlled provision for campers
74   Scafell: enjoyment of the National Park
75   Bowness-on-Windermere: too many visitors?
76   Ullswater: curbing the problem of power boats
77   Coniston Water: carefully managed access
78   Derwent Water: power boats controlled, not prohibited
79   Windermere: regulating the use of boats
80   Hawkshead: bypassed but not relieved
81   Dumped Cars: disposing of rubbish in the National Park
82   Blencathra: John Dower's legacy
83   Raise: provision for skiers
84   Flodder Allotment: importance of nature conservation
85   Aira Force: the rôle of the National Trust in Lakeland
86   Askham: the need for harmony between buildings
87   Windermere: abstraction without damage
88   Satterthwaite: keeping building conversions within limits
89   Ennerdale: wilderness for the walker
90   Chapel Stile: inappropriate ribbon building
91   Windermere: a modern terrace, 'startlingly unattractive'
92   Mosedale: the Lake District's only working mine
93   Central Lake District: a watch on the prominence of farm buildings
94   Aira: nature and extent of the National Park
95   Grasmere: local action to resist pressure for development
96   Dunmail Raise: protecting sheep
97   Stony Cove Pike: farming in the Lake District economy
98   Ennerdale Show: Lake District society
99   Greenside Mines: scars in the landscape
100 Hartsop Valley: carefully studied microcosm
101 Elterwater: slate quarrying
102 Slate Quarry above the Honister Pass: the difficulty of control
103 Copper Mines Valley – quarrying company's proposal defeated
104 Kirkstone Quarries: irresistible pressure of economic activity
105 Limestone Pavement in Orton Area: difficult to protect by law
106 Wastwater: necessity for persistent pressure
107 Ullswater: pollution problems
108 Borrowdale: beauty preserved by supplying electricity underground
109 Seathwaite Valley: development of carefully routed
         electricity supplies
110 Duddon Valley Road near Seathwaite: G.P.O.'s
         consideration for the environment
111 Wasdale: providing an unobtrusive electricity supply

112   Wastwater: laying an electricity supply under water
113   Watendlath: remote; much visited; last hamlet electrified
114   Windscale: a threatening development outside the
          National Park

      Index   205

Preface

Both authors of this book live in Kendal. Geoffrey Berry was appointed Secretary of the Friends of the Lake District in 1966, and in 1976 became its Consultant Secretary. Geoffrey Beard has been Director of the Visual Arts Centre at Lancaster University since 1972. Whilst there has been much collaboration in research and discussion, the two parts of this book have been set out by each author as follows. Geoffrey Beard has written the chapters in Part One that deal with the early years, the development of water supply, afforestation, roads, tourism, and industry. Geoffrey Berry has taken almost all the photographs and written the Conclusion to Part One and the detailed notes contained in Part Two.

The Lake District is an almost unrivalled assemblage of spacious waters, great mountains, and deep, lonely valleys. It is bounded on the west by the Irish Sea, on the east by the Pennines, and at the north by the stark majesty of Hadrian's Wall and the Scottish border. The whole area has expansive lakes, the loftiest mountains in England, and is ribboned by some 30 rivers and innumerable streams and becks. With a long history in geological and human terms, the special nature of the countryside is not easily grasped, even after several visits, or a residence of many years.

Man's use of the natural resources of the Lake District in the past 11 decades has posed many threats to its appearance and survival. The authors realize that they have only been able to select from the many issues that might have been discussed. They have had to allude, all too briefly, to several topics, such as farming, farm buildings, and rural housing, which merit detailed consideration. In the case of water abstraction a full account of Manchester Corporation's acquisition of Thirlmere in the 1870s has been provided. It is a story that in all its aspects does not seem to have been told previously, for nothing relevant appears in Henry W. Hodgson's *A Bibliography of the History and Topography of Cumberland and Westmorland* (1968).

The main source for enquiry has been the extensive archives of the amenity body Friends of the Lake District, founded in 1934. The authors are indebted to its Committee for permission to use material from minute books and news-letters, as well as to consult the large holding of literature issued by other organizations in its possession.

Kendal, February 1979

Geoffrey Berry
Geoffrey Beard

Abbreviations
C.P.R.E.   Council for the Preservation of Rural England
D.o.E.   Department of the Environment
F.L.D.   Friends of the Lake District

PART ONE

I *Early Years of 'Rash Assault'*

It may be that the railway system has extended the trade in the destruction of wild flowers and ferns.

Westmorland Gazette 18 July 1885

When Daniel Defoe, writing in his *A Tour Through the Whole Island of Great Britain* (1724–6), came to his description of Westmorland he found it 'a country eminent only for being the wildest, most barren and frightful of any that I have passed over in England, or even in Wales it self'. He was one of the less respectful of those visitors, who since the late 17th century had travelled to the Lakes in search of dramatic scenery and solitude. These early excursionists, such as Celia Fiennes in the late 17th century, and Thomas Gray in 1769, had crossed the perilous, shifting sands of Morecambe Bay, with horse and phaeton, led by a guide. They thus arrived in the southern Lake District, two of a whole band of water colourists, poets, curious noblemen, and their tired ladies who came north, intent on recording and drawing, or merely revelling, in the natural wonders around them.

The 18th century had seen a great change in English landscape tastes in the substitution of irregularity for formality. Lake and hill, parterre and stream were so arranged that the eye was led what Hogarth in *The Analysis of Beauty* (1753) called 'a wanton kind of chase'. In following the winding walks and serpentine rivers, and adopting new canons of acceptance for linear values, the 18th-century landscapists and water colourists were inevitably influenced in an age weary of formality. There was also a change in the relationship between town and country which came about as a result of increasing urbanization and the effects of the scientific and industrial revolutions. And where there had once been derision for the charms of contrived landscape, mountain gloom, and beauty effective in a picture – the picturesque – acceptance became almost universal.

In treading the many lake-shore paths girt with the herbaceous extravaganzas of Victorian planters we need to keep two significant developments in mind. The 18th-century search for the picturesque delights of the Lake District, which were also being set out in measured stanzas by the Lake poets as the years wore on, and the background of landed patronage that led inexorably to settlements of various levels of a population. There was a mood of expansion abroad, facilitated by the coming of the railway to Windermere (1847). A whole new language arose – 'about 4,450 acres; an annual rental of £10,603 exclusive of the mansion; the mineral rights referred to in the attached schedule' – the language of a scramble towards the elevated and occasionally misprinted accolade of a revered place in Burke's *Landed Gentry*, red and fat, on every respectable land-owner's shelf.

The railways grew into an important means of bringing day-trippers to the Lake District. It also encouraged the development of industry, such as iron-ore mining in the Barrow peninsula and the carriage of slate and stone from various otherwise inaccessible locations.[1] From the 1870s, combined rail-and-steamer trips were being arranged from the Lancashire resorts. Visitors crossed Morecambe bay by steamer, much more comfortably and safely than earlier travellers. The volume of excursion traffic continued to grow in the later 19th century as wages rose and more free time was won. It has been shown that on Whit Monday 1883 about 10,000 day-trippers visited Windermere, of whom 8,000 were brought by the Kendal railway and 2,000 by the Furness line and its steamers.[2]

In the Lake District there had been early fears of the disasters the Kendal and Windermere Railway would bring by encouraging large numbers of day-trippers to venture there from industrial Lancashire. Wordsworth gave passionate expression to his views on many occasions.[3] He was unable to share the near-contemporary opinion of Miss Harriet Martineau who settling at Ambleside in the mid 19th century felt the railroad to be 'the best as well as the last and greatest change in the Lake District'. Both views are in essence allowable. Wordsworth, representative of the many 'gentry' families to settle in the Lake District (or to have a villa there for frequent visits), worried that with no spot free from the 'rash assault' of day-trippers the rural scenes he knew and loved would change for the worse. Miss Martineau saw advantages to trade, property, education, and perhaps even 'an abolition of the town evils of squalor and poor health which harbour in the very heart of the mountains'.[4] Others, with less enlightened views, did not want throngs of curious sightseers peering over their carefully-planted shrubs at strange games of croquet and at well-clad reclining figures in new-fangled deck chairs.

It was obvious however that mineral and other extractors would see value in providing railways to carry ore or slate to market. Attention focused in 1881–3 on the proposal for a railway extension to serve the slate quarries at Honister. Despite its seeming improbability it made some economic sense, and in 1883 a 'Braithwaite and Buttermere Railway Bill' was proposed in Parliament.[5] Slate was to be carried at three pence per ton per mile. Whilst the arguments over the Honister line were proceeding, there were moves in 1883 to provide a railway to carry iron ore out of Ennerdale. But the enabling Bill was thrown out, only to be revived in amended form the following year, and again defeated.

Such actions gave urgency to the formation of an English Lake District Association which had strong representation from Windermere and Bowness hoteliers from the start. It felt, oddly to many, that direct opposition to the railway was beyond its purpose. Significant support was forthcoming from the Lord Chief Justice, from Robert Browning, Alfred Lord Tennyson, Matthew Arnold and John Ruskin, and from the 'Lake District Defence Society' which had been set up to counteract mineral extraction in particular.[6]

One of the declared aims of the English Lake District Association was to maintain existing roads and footpaths in good order. Such activity loomed large in its affairs, but it also lobbied against the picking of wild flowers and ferns, and joined forces with the landowers to oppose, successfully, the extension of the Windermere railway to Ambleside. Four or five issues were to dominate its activities in the late years of Queen Victoria's reign. One of the constant pre-occupations was the filthy sanitary condition of Lake Windermere.[7] In 1876 it had been pronounced that the lake was among the purest drinking waters of England, a position soon lost as tourism increased. In 1879 the English Lake District Association amalgamated with the Lake District Advertising Association to publicize and open out the Lake District, with all that it involved.[8]

It was these efforts to publicize rather than conserve that widened the gap between the Association and the Lake District Defence Society. And its original interest in such subjects as footpaths also waned after 1885 when the Kendal and District Footpaths Preservation Society came into existence.[9] Early in 1885 public indignation had been roused in Keswick by two landowners closing important footpaths near their properties. It was an ill-advised action because as early as 1856 Keswick had a Footpaths Association, and this latest action prompted its revival under the leadership of Canon H. D. Rawnsley, an ardent campaigner for Lake District rights. To settle the footpaths dispute involved some 80 meetings; and finally, in 1887, 2,000 people walked up Latrigg to traverse the disputed paths. Meetings were held in London, Oxford, Manchester, Liverpool, Birmingham, Bristol, and elsewhere. Committees were formed to raise funds to cover legal expenses. And so much publicity was given that the affair became one of almost national interest.

The dispute, heard at Carlisle Assizes in July 1888, was settled by consent. Access to Latrigg top was established and the Association had, by the verdict given, established the right of way from Keswick to Skiddaw, through Spooney Green.[10]

In the years that followed matters of this kind were resolved increasingly by determined bands of Lake District enthusiasts. Sometimes in large groups with adequate finance, and sometimes concerned for an individual's interests, they kept a vital and sensible policy alive. By the First World War though, the Defence Society was fading and two of its most active members, Canon Rawnsley and W. H. Wills, had died. The new Lake District Safeguarding Society founded in 1919, led by Eleanor Rawnsley, was limited in membership to those who owned land in the fells. Such solutions as there seemed to be lay with national policies, supported, with total commitment, by local groups.

The National Park movement in Britain, first examined by the Government in 1929, undoubtedly gained much impetus from the earlier creation of National Parks in other countries. Yellowstone in America had been set up in 1872 and the Kruger National Park in South Africa in 1898. Whilst they safeguarded great tracts of land, which it was not feasible to do in England, their attempts at explaining terrain and wild life, and their conservation programmes were well studied and some of the broad principles of organization adopted.

The National Park movement in England however drew strength from more than foreign examples and the early pastellists' concern for landscape. Rock-climbing and hill-walking, practised by pioneers from Alpine climbs and by such intrepid venturers as the Abraham brothers of Keswick, had emerged as popular pursuits in the late 19th century.[11] Strong pressures were exerted on Government by those who wanted to secure freedom of access to mountain and fell-side, and in 1865 the Commons, Open Spaces, and Footpaths Preservation Society had been founded; an early starter among amenity groups. The protests against the building of railways (1840–80s) and the construction of the Thirlmere reservoir in the 1870s (discussed in the next chapter) had been lessons in organizing protest. The National Trust with its Lake District pioneer founders Octavia Hill and Canon H. D. Rawnsley, had been set up in 1895 by the desire of such individuals to preserve and use sensibly tracts of land and water such as the Lake District.

In the early 1930s the ageing Gordon Wordsworth, always an active member of the Lake District Safeguarding Society, asked Kenneth Spence of Sawrey to be its Honorary Secretary. But within three years, with the active support of the Rev. H. H. Symonds, Patrick Abercrombie, Sir Charles Trevelyan, and others, a body with wider interests was proposed. On 22 September 1934 the first meeting of Friends of the Lake District was held at Ellerthwaite, Windermere. The Society was able to build on the long tradition of maintaining a careful watch on schemes that seemed to threaten the landscape.

The philosophy and concept of National Parks in England was supported enthusiastically by the new organization. But it was to be many years before any seminal work on the concept emerged, with the publication in 1945 of John Dower's study.[12] The 'Hobhouse Committee' was set up to examine Dower's far-reaching proposals and reported in 1947 (Cmd 7121). The themes of preservation of the countryside, access, and wildlife conservation, so important to the Lake District pioneers and developed over some 60 years, continued to influence the thinking that led to the National Parks and Access to the Countryside Act 1949.

This Act established the National Parks Commission and made provision for the future designation of National Parks in England and Wales, provision for nature conservation and nature reserves, and provision for public access to open country. Its powers were reinforced and extended in the Countryside Act 1968, and very effective examination of the position was given in 1974 by the important National Parks Policies Review Committee under Lord Sandford's chairmanship.

In the Lake District the economic needs of the inhabitants of the area, facilities for visitors, and conservation of the landscape have to be balanced. Some control over these became possible when the Lake District was designated as a National Park in 1951 with the aims of preserving and enhancing its natural beauty and promoting its enjoyment by the public. In the same year the Lake District Planning Board was set up as the National Park Authority. As well as its National Park duties the Planning Board as Local Planning Authority had responsibility for the social and economic life of the area.[13]

This study concerns itself with the attempts made to reconcile these often conflicting concerns, and the part played by the amenity bodies in influencing decisions in order to save a few corners of Wordsworth's England. In his *Sonnet on the Projected Kendal and Windermere Railway* 1844, Wordsworth assumed that no nook of English ground was secure from 'rash assault'. The railway he warned about has declined in importance – it could make no effective inroads into mountainous terrain[14] – but its place has been taken by the motor car, and for freight by the heavy lorry. Both raise problems which show, alas, few signs of abating.

II   *The Water of Mammon*

'Now where shall we go' said Dobbs.
'Let's go to Switzerland, this sort of thing' said Potts, climbing
mountaineer-like on to a chair and table, with a broomstick held high.
After debating on Paris – Potts demonstrating an agile high can-can
kick the meanwhile – the two travellers determined finally to go to the
English Lakes, for as Dobbs said:
'Let us see them before they are all turned into reservoirs.'

Adapted from J. Priestman Atkinson *A Week at the Lakes* (1878)

In 1878 the rumours of Manchester's interest in abstracting water from Thirlmere were abroad, and Priestman Atkinson illustrated a 'Fancy Sketch of Thirlmere by a Manchester Artist' showing the lake ringed with factory chimneys and with smoking tug-boats plying its length. The careful conservationists of the time, small band that they were, but ably led by Canon H. D. Rawnsley, had already noticed at least three years earlier, in June 1875, that Manchester Water-works Committee had before it a proposal to abstract water from Ullswater and Haweswater 'in conjunction with Liverpool or independently'. The Royal Commission on Water Supply of 1868 had pronounced with some firmness on the suitability of Ullswater as a water-gathering ground, and Haweswater was adjudged 'similar'. But the Manchester water engineers were canny. Ullswater was 56 ft lower than Thirlmere and pumping would therefore be necessary to supply the city. Using Thirlmere would take advantage of a gravity flow and avoid an added problem, as Ullswater was largely surrounded by residential property that it would have had to purchase. Ullswater could be held in reserve; at Thirlmere there were only a few sheep-farmers to deal with. Also that well-read and beloved Journal *Punch* in 1883 announced, with tongue in cheek, that: 'A lake's a very useless thing' unless its water be taken in pipes to towns. 'As reservoir for waterworks' said the anonymous wag 'some little good it yields. If not it should be drained and made remunerative fields.' Some would believe it and adopt it as a despoiler's text.

Manchester and Liverpool found it difficult to agree, and with Thirlmere eagerly in its sights, Manchester bought the lake and gathering grounds, then applied to Parliament in 1877 for powers of control. John Harwood, the Manchester Waterworks Committee Chairman, wrote to the press in December 1877: 'we have already bought the property . . . to avoid the immeasurably greater cost of compulsory purchase by arbitration. We paid no unreasonable price.' By the Manchester Corporation Water Works Act 1879 they obtained power to raise almost £3½ million, and through an aqueduct extract 50 million gallons of water a day from Thirlmere.

It is an English trait that opposition to bold plundering schemes comes only at a late hour. The considerable publicity about Manchester's intentions led to the summoning of a meeting at Grasmere, and the hurried formation of the Thirlmere Defence Association with a subscription list of £1,000.[15] Robert Crewdson of Rydal Mount and young Robert Somervell of the Kendal shoe-making family put practised pens to paper. Somervell's pamphlets now asked Parliament to consider if the need to extract from Thirlmere was urgent, and if it was the only possible source.[16]

With the active interest of Octavia Hill and Canon Rawnsley, two of the founders of The National Trust, together with the support of William Forster, a member of Gladstone's government, and others in important positions, the campaign was intensified. Within Manchester itself an active lobby forced a poll of ratepayers in 1878, but the result, naturally enough, was a high proportion in favour of an easily acquired water supply.[17] The Thirlmere Defence Association meanwhile had also attracted the attention of two more Members of Parliament, of William Morris, Thomas Carlyle, John Ruskin (who settled at Brantwood on the east bank of Coniston Water in 1871), and of several Oxford and Cambridge dons. The Bishop of Carlisle, Harvey Goodwin, also wrote to *The Times* to say that Thirlmere was free from villas and all that was villainous in an area of primitive and untouched beauty. 'Shall we hear' he wrote 'of a month at the Reservoirs?'[18]

The aged Ruskin wrote further that 'Manchester is plotting to steal the waters of Thirlmere and the clouds of Helvellyn'.[19] Those with lesser reputations did not hesitate before joining in, on either side, but it was the protesters with letters and entreaties to action who were the most persistent. Canon Rawnsley, already saddened that Manchester was turning 'shapely Thirlmere into tanks' found it a real grief 'to see the raw soil embankments scarring the sides of the fells.'[20] He knew that the quiet footpaths, which Matthew Arnold had described in his poem 'Resignation', must soon be flooded and the old bridge at the Narrows (at this time Thirlmere had two reaches joined by narrows which were bridged) would be known no more. Then came the news that the 'Rock of Names', the trysting-place of the Lake poets, was to be broken up and the stone used for the walls of the waterworks. On this rock were graven the initials of six friends – Wordsworth, his affianced bride Mary Hutchinson, his sister Dorothy Wordsworth, Samuel Taylor Coleridge, John Wordsworth, and Sarah Hutchinson. Rawnsley obtained permission to move it, but the task proved impossible. When the rock was blown to pieces by dynamite, Rawnsley and his wife collected fragments, and under his direction these were built into the cairn that stands on the east side of the road to Keswick at a higher level.

The construction of the road on the western side of Thirlmere was opposed in 1889 by the Lake District Defence Association. For two or three years local people had worried about the heavy stone carting by Manchester Corporation's workmen which was damaging the road between Ambleside and Keswick. They wondered whether this great Authority was to be allowed to block the main road and to bear no part of the costs of maintenance.[21] A more emotive ratepayer had joined in, and had written to the *Westmorland Gazette*:

avaunt, ye votaries of Mammon! – ye artisans unwashed! Keep to your industries, and leave us our sublime scenery.[22]

Negotiations over the Thirlmere scheme were prolonged and difficult[23] – some of Manchester's aldermen hoped (in vain) for a visit by the Prince of Wales to smooth the way.[24] The Corporation was patient, though, and it says much for the astute way Corporation officials handled the later stages of charge and counter-charge that at the final opening on 12 October 1894, Canon Rawnsley was asked to open the proceedings with prayer. Later he was called upon to propose the toast to the Waterworks Committee: he added a note of appreciation to Manchester. The waters of Thirlmere were thus harnessed to slake distant thirst, and to serve the impatient clattering mills in Lancashire.

It may well be thought that such an ardent campaigner for the preservation of the Lake District as Rawnsley should not have acted as he did. However, a careful reading of all the evidence shows that the Thirlmere campaign was really waged by others.[25] Rawnsley always owned that he recognized the demands of a great city of working-men for pure water, and that he had never written or spoken against the undertaking. Whilst this was not strictly accurate – he had lamented in the *Pall Mall Gazette* in 1887 'Thirlmere, magical in loveliness, is doomed' – it was one of his few periods of inactivity.

What the Manchester scheme did to Thirlmere in impounding it for a reservoir was to deal a heavy blow to natural beauty. All lakes by natural processes dam themselves with silt and stones. Even in the driest weather no lake falls below the lip of its own natural dam, and in the stormiest weather will only rise a foot or two for a few days until the surplus water has run off. Within these limits of slight change the shore edge is a constant point, where vegetation, water, and the washed pebbles meet in a natural harmony. Dam a lake artificially and the face of nature is changed. In dry weather the insistent draw-off through distant taps brings down the water level far below the new and artificial shore line. Thirlmere, with its edge of conifers, has been like this on many occasions, giving to its shores the ugly hard lines that appear at time of drought.

The successful incursion made by Manchester into Lake District sources for its water supply did not go unnoticed by others.[26] It was inevitable that the towns of western Cumbria, Workington and Whitehaven, should look eastwards to the greater lakes when local resources proved inadequate. As early as 1899 Workington was interested in Crummock Water, and the various Private Acts of Parliament it obtained, serve as a sombre record of its persistent water abstraction at Crummock, Ennerdale, and Wastwater. By early Acts of 1849 and 1859 the Whitehaven Town and Harbour Trustees had been given powers to take water from Ennerdale Water. Powerful agencies were always ready to come forward, and Whitehaven and Workington had noted that just before the second reading of the 'Thirlmere Bill' the Prince of Wales had indicated that 'great good might arise from open discussion of water supplies. The larger populations are striving, each independently and at enormous cost to secure water. We should consider a comprehensive national scheme for the wants of the districts'.[27] The need for water continued unabated.

In 1919 by a Private Act of Parliament, Manchester was empowered to buy the watersheds of Mardale, Swindale, and Wet Sleddale – 24,000 acres. In the original Bill it was proposed to extinguish the traditional rights of access over all this area. The Commons, Open Spaces and Footpaths Preservation Society which had been set up in 1865 managed to have a clause (no. 43) inserted as part of the Act, by which the public were given full right of 'air, exercise and recreation' on all the common land and all the unenclosed land then acquired, subject to by-laws in control of conduct.[28]

However work was long delayed at Haweswater. It did not begin until 1929, and was held up during the financial depression of 1931, except for the making of the tunnels. By 1934 the Manchester Waterworks Committee had decided to construct the dam to raise the lake level. Water consumption had increased since work had started, and a drought in the summer of 1934 gave urgency to raising the dam to the full height originally suggested, rather than to an interim point. What this meant in human terms, at whatever the level decided, was the flooding of Mardale.

The 'drowned village' of Mardale which sank beneath the rising waters of Haweswater reappears like a shadowy ghost in times of extreme drought, such as the summer of 1976.[29] A quiet corner of Lakeland with a slow pace, with time to stand and stare, and where a rat race 'was a scuffling in the barn roof', Mardale is a symbol of the price that is sometimes paid by the few on behalf of the many. As Lady Simon recorded in her history of Manchester City government, 'we cannot feel, however, that the history of the Haweswater scheme is an example of far-sighted planning at its best'.[30]

This comment is borne out by subsequent events. At the end of 1972 the Water Resources Board published its study of water supplies for the whole of the country to the end of this century. There had been earlier reports concerning schemes in the north-west, including detailed and exhaustive studies of the Morecambe Bay Barrage proposals. The proposals that concerned Lake District conservationists were the enlargement of Haweswater, and new reservoirs in the Borrowbeck valley and at Killington.

At Haweswater the proposal was to raise the height of the dam by 115 ft. The increased capacity of the reservoir would be used by pumping from the River Eden at Staingills, with the water then piped to the River Lune, for abstraction at or near its mouth at Lancaster. Haweswater would thus become, it was stated, 'a regulating reservoir as well as continuing its direct supply function into Manchester's pipelines', and herein lay the threat.[31] River regulation entails great variation in level, particularly in summer. The sides of the Mardale valley are steep and the artificial rise and fall of the water level would have an extensive eroding effect. In addition, the impact of a massive new dam would be severe in the attractive countryside around Bampton and Rosgill. The wooded peninsula of the Rigg would, like Mardale village, almost disappear and the valley floor be further engulfed. Thus it was in 1972 – a scheme presumably sound in its engineering context, but damaging to an attractive part of the National Park. The scale of a reservoir is essentially grand and bold, and civic pride has often been further demonstrated with the erection of Gothic-style pumping houses, castellated dams, and foundation stones chiselled with resounding facts and names.

The Haweswater situation is still a continuing concern. Land-use consultants have reported to the North West Water Authority, which issued a report in January 1979. It was claimed that note had been taken of agricultural, ecological, and social considerations to produce preferred schemes to raise the level of Haweswater, flood Borrowbeck, Tebay, to create a new reservoir, store water in the estuaries of Morecambe Bay, or construct a reservoir at Hellifield. Local authorities would be given six months to comment on the schemes before the Water Authority decided which one to adopt. All the schemes are bound to meet fierce opposition from the conservationist groups and local people.

A fuller study of water extraction in the north-west than we are able to give, taking account of suggested measures for conserving supplies (e.g. dual-flush lavatory systems, metered domestic supplies, industrial recycling) would be a valuable exercise. It is partially done each time a body such as the North West Water Authority, or the National Water Council issues a detailed study.[32] But such pronouncements must be considered in the light of the impact their proposals would make if implemented.

This chapter must conclude with accounts of two further debates over water abstraction – the long battles over Manchester's involvement at Ullswater, and over the interests of Whitehaven and the North West Water Authority at Ennerdale. It is necessary to recite briefly the early facts. When the cities of Liverpool and Manchester needed extra water, they looked towards the Lake District. John Bateman, as consultant engineer to both cities, was asked in the 1870s to advise on obtaining water supplies from there. He proposed that the two cities should have a joint supply to provide 40 million gallons a day to each city. The size of the scheme frightened some of the members of the Manchester Waterworks Committee, but before they could act Liverpool made arrangements for its own supply from North Wales. Manchester, with a considerable problem to solve alone, and with the Lake District its only major source of supply, looked to Haweswater, Ullswater, and Thirlmere. For the reasons mentioned earlier, primarily a gravity flow, Thirlmere was chosen.

In 1961 the House of Lords rejected clauses in Manchester's Private Bill to secure powers over Ullswater.[33] Following the debate a conference was organized under the auspices of the Ministry of Housing and Local Government. The conference set up two groups, a Technical Committee of engineers, and an Amenity Committee of planners, to study the water requirements of Manchester and the north western towns generally, and to report on means for satisfying them.[34] The final report of the conference (which was presided over by Lord Jellicoe) showed clearly that there were a number of alternative schemes, larger or smaller, by which the requirements of the north western towns might be satisfied for a number of years to come, without using lakes or flooding valleys in the Lake District.

The reports, press statements, and evidence from amenity bodies concerning Ullswater alone is substantial. In 1964 Manchester accepted its engineer's report and decided to seek powers to abstract an average of 25 million gallons a day from Ullswater. It was expected that pumps and a pipeline having a capacity of 80 million gallons a day would be installed. There was also expected to be a nodding glance at the possibility of extracting a mere 20 million gallons a day from Windermere. Manchester's Water Order was issued in January 1965 in the terms outlined above, but with a suggestion that the pumping stations would be underground and earth-covered; their operation, it was promised, would be virtually noiseless. It was proposed also to construct a duplicate of the Mardale tunnel, by laying 48 in. diameter watermains down the entire valley bottom in Longsleddale.

The work at Ullswater was calculated to take three years, and the impressive array of mobile cranes, compressors, excavators, dumpers, pipe transporters, workmen's buses, Land Rovers, and muck carts needed could then only be visualized as a distant threat. The inevitable public inquiry opened in Kendal on 1 June 1965 and continued without interruptions until 9 July. Manchester supported, with a wealth of figures, her contention that the needs of the undertaking, now in effect a regional water authority, were 'urgent and desperate'. But the objectors, in Parliament (led principally by Lord Birkett) and outside, saw in Manchester's proposals the thin end of what might become a very large wedge.

It took a year for the Minister to issue his decision after the public inquiry. He accepted Manchester's plea of urgency and over-ruled the careful arguments of the 14 amenity bodies represented. The Minister endeavoured to hedge round his permission with various checks and restrictions.[35] He made it clear that he had been deeply impressed with the apprehensions voiced on behalf of the objectors – fears that Manchester, as in the past, would, like Oliver Twist come back, for more. But the Manchester Water Order 1966 was in being. The collection and presentation of evidence for the inquiry by the Council for the Preservation of Rural England (C.P.R.E.), the National Trust, and others cost some £11,000, a sum hard to garner again to meet the next serious threat.

Early in 1947 Whitehaven Corporation (then a Water Authority), following a public inquiry held in the previous year, obtained confirmation of a Water Order giving them powers to re-embank and raise Ennerdale Water. At the time, owing to the failure of plans to establish a rayon factory near by, the Water Order was held in abeyance. By 1962 industrial expansion in west Cumberland brought the threat of implementing the 1947 Order a little nearer, and mention was made of raising the lake level by 4½ ft.[36]

To look along the length of Ennerdale Water towards Pillar is to see one of the finest lake-and-mountain views in England. Ennerdale is a wild and dramatic place. The afforestation of the valley floor has not tamed its upper reaches, no building stands upon the lake shore, and no motor road reaches beyond its entrance. It must be explored on foot; no other Lake District valley remains in this state of primitive beauty.

In 1978 the North West Water Authority proposed a £2.2 million scheme to raise the level of Ennerdale Water – its favourite scheme amongst the several proposed in its 1976 report *Water Resources in Cumbria*. It was also £1.8 million cheaper than abstraction from near the mouth of the River Derwent, at Workington.

These may seem significant statistics until one notes that 'improving' the A66 cost £32 million, and it is planned to spend over £600 million on the extension of the nuclear plant at Windscale. Something will have gone seriously wrong with our sense of values if this country can afford sums of that magnitude, and yet be unable to afford £2 million to save a unique valley in the country's premier National Park.

The Forestry Commission is working on plans to improve the appearance of the Ennerdale forests; the hard lines of the upper boundaries will be broken to a more natural appearance, and selective felling will ease the blanket of uniform spruce. It would be ironical if one authority's efforts to enhance the beauty of the dale were countered by the damaging work of another. The chess-play move and counter-move is in progress towards a major public inquiry.* The Ennerdale scheme is supported in principle by Cumbria County Council, and to varying degrees opposed by at least nine amenity bodies and the Countryside Commission, the National Trust (the Lake District's largest landowner), Copeland Borough Council, and Allerdale District Council.

The Water Act of 1973 (Section 22) imposed duties on the Water Authority to have regard to amenity and nature conservation in carrying out its duties. The Water Resources Act of 10 years earlier (1963) required that such an Authority in the exercise of its functions should 'have regard to the character of the inland water and its surroundings (and, in particular, any natural beauty which the inland water and its surroundings may possess)'. A long, and no doubt expensive struggle lies ahead against this further attempt to turn Ennerdale, one of the most attractive lakes, into a major reservoir in a National Park.

* The Public Inquiry opened at Whitehaven on 15 January, 1980 whilst this book was in production. Its scope was extended to consider proposed abstraction from Wastwater by British Nuclear Fuels Ltd.

III   *The Coniferous Mass*

It is therefore impossible, under any circumstances, for the artificial planter to rival the beauty of Nature.

William Wordsworth *Guide to the Lakes* (1835)

In the third section of Wordworth's *Guide to the Lakes* there are some very firm criticisms of the spread of Ornamental Gardening in the early 19th century. Ever concerned about harshness in the landscape the poet's views on suitable materials for, and colour of, buildings, exotic trees, planting fashions and undisturbed prospects are still apt and relevant. But before these trenchant observations were made, Thomas Gray had visited the Lakes, in 1769, and had commented on Wythop Brows on the western side of Bassenthwaite Lake as 'being clothed to the top with wood'.[37] John Housman, visiting in 1802, set out all he had seen in a verbosely-titled book. He noted that a Mr Story was rearing plantations of larch on the eastern shores of Bassenthwaite, and that his efforts on the rocky front of the barren mountain ought to encourage similar attempts[38] in many other parts of Cumberland and Westmorland 'to turn the almost useless hills to advantage and beautify the country by planting them with trees'.[39]

The Lakes were already a fashionable visiting spot and there were those who having once been captivated by majestic scenery settled down to live there.[40] And on living there, and considering it sound commercial or aesthetic practice, they started to set out the plantations of larch. Chief amongst them was Richard Watson, Bishop of Llandaff, who lived at Calgarth on the eastern shore of Lake Windermere – some of the woods he created about 1790 are still named Bishop Wood or Bishop Plantation. A few years later the Governors of Greenwich Hospital, after they had acquired property at Keswick which had belonged to the Earl of Derwentwater (beheaded in 1716), did a great deal of planting. As well as hardwoods they planted Scots pine and larch and were much abused and criticized for doing so. It was noted in 1943 that a dozen larches planted by them were felled in 1942, and that the rings showed annual growth for more than 140 years.[41]

Wordsworth did not like the larch – 'ten thousand of this spiky tree, the larch, are stuck in at once upon the side of a hill: they can grow up into nothing but deformity' he wrote.[42] The receipts from quick-growing coppices of larch, spruce, and pine had however always been an important factor in the economy of a country estate.[43] In the Lake District they were sold to feed the eager machinery of the extensive bobbin-making industry and, after burning, as charcoal for the gunpowder mills of Westmorland and Furness.[44] In addition

13

the manufacture of tool handles, brush stocks, barrels, baskets, pencils, and pill boxes made heavy demands on many sources of timber.

The first large-scale afforestation in the Lake District however was that undertaken by Manchester in 1908 to protect the catchment area of its reservoir at Thirlmere. Spread over nearly 2,000 acres the formal firs with their unsocial shade now cling to the valley sides in all directions. It was this uniformity and regularity to which, in his own day, Wordsworth objected. Continued planting of conifers alarmed preservationists into action by the threat they posed to the unique character of the Lake District. The Forestry Commission was the main object of their wrath. It had a near monopoly in planting.

When Wordsworth wrote of 'tens of thousands' of larches he probably assumed that was the limit of rash planting. But by the end of September 1933 the Forestry Commission had already planted in the Lake District nearly one and a quarter million larches, and over five million spruce.[45] They were set out in Ennerdale, and on the Thornthwaite Estate, some 5,000 acres near Keswick which they had developed since 1920.[46] The Norway spruce or 'Christmas tree' gave a rapid growth of timber in the prevailing damp climate, but in exposed situations its place in the planting cycle was gradually taken by the North American Sitka spruce. The acquisition of land in upper Eskdale by the Forestry Commission in 1933 finally triggered the mounting concern. The Friends of the Lake District (F.L.D.) in 1934 decided to contact the Commission with a view to persuading them to plant as much hardwood as possible, to safeguard rights of way, and grant future access.[47] The Commission's record on hardwood planting was not good: of the land afforested, as distinct from that reafforested, 1,144 acres in Ennerdale had been planted with conifers, and 1,308 acres on the Thornwaite estate, while the area planted with broadleaved species amounted to only 18 acres in Ennerdale and 17 in Thornthwaite.[48]

The novelist Hugh Walpole, who lived in the Lake District at the time and had made it the scene of some of his best-known novels, wrote to *The Times* to protest that the planting of Eskdale 'with larch and spruce is to ruin it once and for ever'.[49] The case by the many objectors against softwoods was basically this: a) they were not native to the country; b) they were not as pleasing to the eye as indigenous hardwoods; and c) the 'blanketing of vast areas of open fell by uniform fir forests destroyed the varied contours and open spaces which constituted the special beauty of the district'. There was also considerable feeling against the enclosure of wild fell land which had been habitually open to the public by the courtesy of its owners and farmers. Afforestation also required the displacement of sheep and the abandonment of ancient sheep-farms; moreover by the provisions of the Forestry Act in 1919 the Commission had powers of compulsory purchase.

In a difficult atmosphere lengthy discussions started between the Commission and the C.P.R.E. The Commission on its 7,000 acres wanted to set out the 'Hardknott Forest Park' over the choicest parts of Eskdale and Dunnerdale. Conflict with the amenity groups was inevitable and behind the scenes activity was intense. It culminated in a petition of 13,000 names presented to the Commissioners in September 1935 which also set out an area within the Lake

District in which, it was suggested, no planting should take place. The C.P.R.E., supported by many bodies such as the National Trust and F.L.D., had combined in firm but reasoned argument, and both Symonds, as Treasurer of F.L.D., and John Dower (a member of its Committee, and later author of an important report instrumental in setting up National Parks)[50] were at the heart of the long campaign. Dower prepared maps showing areas which it was suggested should be protected from encroachment, and in April 1936 a deputation was organized to meet the Commission. It was headed by the Archbishop of York, and included the Vice-Chancellor of Oxford University (Lord Balniel), the Bishop of Peterborough, Sir Arthur Somervell, and Norman Birkett, who throughout his life was to play many important rôles in safeguarding the Lake District. Dower's map had its areas of preservation reduced in size, and he stated in July 1936, at a time when the Joint Committee's White Paper was about to be issued,[51] that it was quite clear to him that the Commission 'were no more prepared to grant the requests in full than when they had answered the deputation in June'.[52] Lord Howard of Penrith even suggested that the executive of F.L.D. should press for a Private Members' Bill to set up a commission similar to that of the Fine Arts Commission to consider matters of preservation over the whole of Great Britain. Tempers often flared beyond control.

However the combined efforts of the 10-year old C.P.R.E (founded 1926) and the two-year old F.L.D. (founded 1934) resulted finally in an uneasy agreement, which bound the Commission not to acquire any land for afforestation in the central 300 sq. miles of the Lake District. It had been a long and involved struggle and some of its complex pattern has been reported on at least three occasions; once as it happened in 1936, again in 1955, and once more, 40 years after the original talks, in a useful statement on the politics of pressure.[53]

One of the main problems left by the 1936 'agreement' was 'shaded areas', in map terms, in Eskdale, Dunnerdale, and Ennerdale which, whilst subject to special considerations, were outside the 'black line' protected area. The C.P.R.E. representatives regretted this and recorded their disagreement with the Commission in the 1936 White Paper.[54]

The National Trust had not been directly concerned with the controversy but had taken great interest in it. It then owned some 12,000 acres in the three Lake Counties (Lancashire, Westmorland, Cumberland) and had a large area of woodland in its care. It had acquired Brandelhow Park by subscription as early as 1902, consisting mostly of oak woods on the lower slopes of Cat Bells. The Trust owned other woodlands on its Derwent Water estates, and at Ullswater its large Gowbarrow property was beautifully wooded, with oak, alder, birch, and mountain ash. Between the Lake and the waterfall, Aira Force, was the Pinetum where many splendid trees had flourished since their planting by the Howards of Greystoke.

By the mid thirties, however, the Trust's most extensive woodlands were at, or near, Tarn Hows, between Coniston and Hawkshead. These woods were part of the Monk Coniston estate planted by the Marshall family. In 1935 the Trust also acquired as a result of public subscription nearly all the woods at Buttermere, Crummock Water, and Loweswater. Larch and spruce were liberally established on this property but not in sufficient numbers to blanket the slopes. In quantity elsewhere they had threatened the unique character of the Lake District – a coniferous and spiky mass.

The 1936 agreement, with its black-line area, had included the high wild part of Eskdale. Two ancient sheep-farms at Brotherikeld, at the head of Eskdale, and Black Hall at the head of the Duddon, were destined to become part of the 'Hardknott Forest Park'. The Commissioners were urged in 1938 to enter into covenants with the National Trust, but for their part they required compensation at the rate of £2 an acre for the 740 acres in Eskdale which they had intended to afforest. Also the Commission had persistently refused to exclude from commercial afforestation the Duddon valley, lying in the southern Lake District.

To protect the farm land of High Wallabarrow, threatened with purchase by the Commission, the farm was bought privately in 1938, placed under restrictive covenant, and passed on at an economic price to Lake District Farm Estates for permanent protection.[55] A successful subscription was also raised by F.L.D. in 1940 to outbid the Commission for 300 acres of fell land below High Wallabarrow. The object was to stop commercial planting and have 'a compact protective holding in this lovely part of the Duddon Valley, where it opens widely out in the area below the gorge'.[56]

Controversy over the Hardknott estate raged on into the early days of the Second World War. The form of covenant with the National Trust could not be agreed, and only a temporary settlement seemed possible in 1943, by designating the land as a 'National Forest Park'. A Forestry Commission committee was set up, and it reported in 1945 that an area of some 827 acres of Commission land in Eskdale would be retained in its natural state with reasonable public access 'to and across a further area of approximately five thousand acres of higher fell land which is unplantable'.[57] There were those who held that the Forestry Commission had little right to the possession of 5,000 acres which were unplantable, and which moreover, as the Committee's report acknowledged, was an area of national importance for mountaineers and fell-walkers. The Hardknott Forest Park was closed finally in 1959 as the remaining forest area was insufficient in area to justify the title.

In 1936 the Commissioners had undertaken to pay special attention to amenity in afforesting the plantable ground in Duddondale and in Eskdale, including the use of broad leaved trees on suitable land. Unfortunately, in some areas of great scenic beauty there is often little 'suitable land' and thus opportunity for a casual policy arises. However, the Commission were to observe care in the lay out of rides and boundaries. By 1945 the message had been sufficiently stated for special attention to be paid, at least on the printed page, to 'the amenity aspect', including such matters as:

a. planting of such species as will give the greatest possible natural effect consistent with good forestry

b. avoidance of hard outline edges to the plantations which should follow natural contours as much as possible

c. leaving unplanted the viewpoints and so much of the surrounding land as will enable the view to be enjoyed when the trees have grown

d. protecting the skylines by not planting too close to them

e. keeping planting well back from both sides of the Hardknott road and refraining from planting between that road and the becks that run parallel to its course on the north side of the ascent from the Wrynose bottom

f. restricting planting so that the plantations are not close down to the sides of the Gaitscale and Mosedale Gills, and generally speaking leaving free of trees the rock formations and banks of streams

g. preservation of the sylvan element in the landscape of the Eskdale dale-head.[58]

Fine words, but it took some a long time to overlook the earlier statements made during the war years. In November 1942 the Forestry Commission said that it took full responsibility for not implementing the rigid 1936 agreement.[59] In September 1943 the F.L.D. Committee noted the damage done by the Commission in the Duddon valley to hill-farming by the stopping up of drift-roads and restricting access.[60] But they were war years, in which little could be achieved, and it was easy to cite national expediency to cover bad decisions.

In 1951 the F.L.D. Committee decided to reissue a reprint of the 1936 agreement made between the Forestry Commission and the C.P.R.E. They had assumed that the 1951 Forestry Act might well lead to some difficulty, and discussions were soon in progress to reach agreed amendments. The Commission pointed out that under immediate post-war economic conditions some owners of private woodland found it difficult to maintain it properly, or to afford the costs of replanting. If such woodlands were not to become derelict three courses seemed worth discussion. The owner could accept replanting grants, on a scale fixed under the powers of the Act, for a scheme of replanting approved by the Forestry Commission. He could enter into a 'dedication covenant' with the Commission, which in effect meant the assumption of management by the Commission. And finally, if the owner was unwilling to co-operate with the Commission in either of these ways, the Forestry Acts provided for the Commission itself to acquire and manage the woodlands.

It was here that the Commission was brought up against the 1936 Agreement. Three hundred sq. miles of the Central Lake District had been 'ruled out altogether from afforestation' by the Commission, which undertook not to acquire land within the central area, and also to consult the C.P.R.E. on proposed planting operations in certain important areas to the south of this central block.

Nobody who valued the beauty of the Lake District wanted to see existing private woodlands become derelict, so there was an obvious case for some relaxation of the full rigour of the 1936 position. In edging carefully into the debate again F.L.D. had three objectives before it; firstly, to preserve the 'open country' of the central Lake District for general rambling access; secondly, to preserve the character of the Lake District scene, largely created by its scattered woodlands of native trees, by preventing these from being replaced by conifer forests; and thirdly, to protect, and to foster, the traditional occupation of fell-farming by continuing the use of the fell-sides for rough grazing, instead of for afforestation, and of the valley bottoms as pasture and meadow.[61]

The National Trust was now the largest single owner of private woodland within the central area, and an immediate concern of the 1954 negotiations was the ill effects which might well follow if a Deed of dedication between the Commission and National Trust reserved to the Trust too little say in the planting policy to be adopted. By December 1954 a satisfactory solution seemed to have been worked out. It was provided in the 1955 Amendment to the 1936 Agreement that the Commission should 'not be debarred from acquiring wood-land areas which were under timber trees in 1936', and further that the maintenance and restocking of these areas should be with 'the hardwood trees characteristic of the Lake District scene'.[62] Certain areas of special scenic beauty 'where this objective cannot reasonably be attained may possibly not be replanted at all'. Oil poured steadily on to troubled waters by the further agreement that if some softwood planting had to be done in the acquired woodlands the changes to the traditional scene would be kept to the minimum. Moreover, the Commission undertook to consult the C.P.R.E. on those occasions when it acquired woodland under the amended arrangements.

During the war some National Trust woodland at Loweswater and Buttermere was requisitioned by the Ministry of Supply and parts of it were clear-felled. Larch was cut and a problem arose in considering its replacement. Clear-felling, as opposed to selective felling, makes it impossible not to replant in straight lines. The young trees need to be kept free of undergrowth, and this is not easily possible if the new trees are scattered about at random, making them difficult to find and clear.

The aim is always selective felling (inside fences which are maintained as sheep-proof) with natural regeneration or new planting, or both, in the open spaces so left. This is in fact nature's own method of forest maintenance; the trees, as they reach maturity and fall, replace themselves by self-seeding, and the wood has a continuous life as an organic whole, the trees being of uneven ages and (almost always) of varied species. Such a policy, if followed by men, not only ends the problem of straight-line planting; it also ends the objections to the rough and unseemly scars on hillsides, which clear-felling must always leave and which take many years to heal. Indeed, when there is clear-felling, critics of afforestation cannot escape the two-edged comment that they object equally – though in fact they object with equal cause – when a wood is cut down, and when it is replanted with trees of a kind not suited to the landscape.

On the far shore of Loweswater the two main points of criticism were that, firstly, on the higher levels of the fell there had been too much replanting (a part of it, certainly, with oak) and that some of the land would have been better left to revert to fell. Secondly, on the very important flat land by the lake shore too much conifer had been put in, a part of this planting coming right down to the lake shore, which was considered most unsuitable treatment. The National Trust agreed that there should be a firm policy of introducing or carefully regenerating hardwoods (that is, broadleaved trees) wherever the ground was not too wet to carry a final hardwood crop.[63]

The extensive plantations of larch on the west shore of Buttermere, some parts of which were replanted in 1941, showed that any stiffly patterned intrusion is liable to diminish the beauty of the landscape. In 1947 the Hobhouse Committee, established to make recommendations on setting up National Parks (following the pioneer report by John Dower) said of the Lake District woods:

> During the war they have been much felled, especially in the southern dales. The beauty of the Lake District would be sadly diminished if these woods were to be permanently lost or replanted with any but their native trees.[64]

But over 2,800 acres of broadleaved woodland in the National Park about 30 years ago is now predominantly coniferous, with upper Ennerdale dominated by the conifer plantations.[65]

It was presumably with such examples in mind that, when the National Parks and Access to the Countryside Bill became law in 1949, it provided reasons for protecting against afforestation the plantable land which still remained. The Forestry Commission had pursued its policy of making 'fiscal concessions to owners of productive woodland and by planting grants'.[66] This encouraged forestry investment groups which, in various parts of the country, were able to offer high prices for farms coming on the market. This further depressed the desire to carry on hill farming. It led to a strenuous campaign to bring afforestation within the process of formal planning control which, regrettably, did not succeed.[67] The Government's consultative document, *Forestry Policy* (1972) indicated that 'the planting programmes of the Forestry Commission, and Government support for private forestry in future, could be justified only by the creation and maintenance of employment in rural areas that would otherwise be depopulated, and by such amenity value as could be derived from afforestation'. Similar arguments had been advanced in the 1930s by the Government and the Forestry Commission for the relief of unemployment in West Cumberland by its policy of afforestation within the Lake District.[68]

Forestry policies within the Lake District are a complex issue with a long history of antagonism between the Forestry Commission and the amenity bodies.[69] Present relationships are more helpful and constructive, and the efficiency of the Lake District Special Planning Board, and of F.L.D. in particular, does much to monitor the situation and to consider and implement improvements. Reference has been made to the important survey *Broadleaved Woodlands of the Lake District* issued by the Special Planning Board (1978). Its recommendations and the methods outlined to implement them merit wide support:

    a. Sites of special scientific interest (graded I or II in terms of size, species, habitat, diversity etc.) 'should be safeguarded and managed so as to conserve and enhance their wildlife and landscape values'.

b. Outside these sites attempts will be made to maintain the continuity of broadleaved woodland zones, and to see that important individual woods outside the zones are not adversely affected by change.

c. Encouragement will be given to the planting of 'new broadleaved woods, clumps and individual trees, and where appropriate, the diversification of conifer stands'.

And, most vital: 'the conservation of the existing broadleaved woodland should be regarded as the most important aspect of a broad-based approach to trees and woods designed to conserve the natural beauty of the Lake District'. It is an approach the early fighters such as Symonds would have been proud of, and points to a future in which informed criticism and suggestions will be made, considered carefully, and in many cases the outcome implemented.

Significantly the Chairman of the Lakes Council speaking in December 1978 to a joint meeting with the Lake District Special Planning Board urged massive afforestation of the Lake District.[70] He advocated mass replanting of the whole area, with broadleaf trees up to 1,500 ft, and pine trees in the additional 500 ft where broadleaf trees will not grow. Unless this were done he feared the fells would become as bare of soil as the hills of North Wales. Action now would save the countryside 200 years in the future. Whatever the merits of the case it is protection for the future that conservationists fight for, today and tomorrow. They had few harder battles than that for the Lake District woodlands. The reward is the glowing autumn colouring mirrored in the lakes and bright clear tarns.

IV *High and Low Roads*

The alterations upon the road betwixt Kendal and Penrith are of such a magnitude and extent as will soon avoid the steepest and worst parts.

Westmorland Gazette 31 December 1819

When John Ogilby issued his map of Kendal in 1675 he drew in four roads only – from Kendal to Carlisle via Shap; a part-coastal road from Egremont through Whitehaven to Workington, Cockermouth and Bothel to Carlisle; a cross-road from Cockermouth via Keswick and Ambleside to Kendal; and a road between Newcastle and Carlisle. They were soon to prove inadequate for an area expanding with business, especially mining, and eventually tourism. The 1801 Census recorded a population of 117,230 in Cumberland and 40,805 in Westmorland. This represented a 95 per cent increase over the Cumberland population in 1700 of about 60,000, and that in Westmorland was some 36 per cent above the 1700 figure of 27,000. The roads for the most part must have resembled Benjamin Browne's description in 1730–1 of those in the Kendal Ward – 'bad' or 'narrow' or 'covered with ye hedges'.[71]

Slow improvements in administration and expenditure contributed to an increased road network, made necessary by continued suburban growth. It was apparent that in a mountainous area like the Lake District the arteries of road would always outnumber those of rail although the latter were vital to the growth of trade and leisure activities. The railway, after it had reached Windermere in 1847, had induced four main developments. Firstly it attracted commuters and summer residents. This led to an interesting phase of villa development and improvements in social life. Thirdly it created in Windermere and Bowness a new settlement with shopping facilities; and finally it brought many long-stay visitors for a few weeks at the Lakes. The resort was also made more accessible to the middle classes and the working classes, who packed into the steam trains for a day's outing.[72]

The Motor Car Act 1903 required the registration of all motor vehicles, and the honour of the first listing in Cumberland went to William Parkin Moore of Wigton with his 5 hp Baby Peugeot. By the end of 1904 there were 281 cars in the county,[73] and as they chugged along the narrow roads they were joined by those from more distant towns to the south and east. George Abraham, the renowned Keswick mountaineer and photographer, found motoring as exciting as mountaineering.[74] He had a Sunbeam Mabberley with tiller steering, soon to be replaced by a 10 hp Allday. In 1913 he issued *Motor Ways in Lakeland* with memorable understated phrases about his exploits on almost every page: 'the lower part of the Honister Pass road' he wrote 'has several steep little pitches, and one awkward corner rather less than halfway up the ascent'. Most of the mountain roads were unmetalled, and the gradients and corners were steep and sharp. In June 1913, George, in a 10 hp Humber, made the first hazardous crossing of Hardknott and Wrynose Passes from west to east, a route that had defeated a number of more powerful machines. Where he led, others, some-times in foolhardy mood, followed, with their leather helmets and goggles at odds with the slow, chugging, hard-tyred pace. They had progressed from the 'Locomobile' with its fixed gear and diet of Russian paraffin (which the carpet manufacturer Herbert Crossley, living on the west bank of Windermere, used) and could now outpace the paraffin 'buses of the Lake District Road Traffic Company. [75]

The essential Lake District is very small: a circle with a radius of some 15 miles, with its centre near the Langdale Pikes, contains the whole of it. There-fore its mountain grandeur and bracing solitudes are the more easily liable to changes of quality and tone. Foremost in the erosion of the isolation was the motor car: what it needed was drivers, petrol, and ever-wider roads. The conservationists argued in 1934 that whilst they accepted the need for good motor access to the Lake District and its environs, the two or three natural through-routes that existed should, under careful regulations, be maintained, but not increased. All Lake District road widths should remain well below what was normal elsewhere. Certain dale-head roads and passes should remain primitive, and some routes, scarcely passable, should be closed to motor traffic entirely. The slogans were trenchant:

> We are against 'improvement' of the by-roads and mountain trackways in the Lake District. Motorists get more than they ask, and walkers lose what they need. Leave the passes for walkers. Leave the by-roads untarred. Leave the grass verges. No more grants from the Ministry of Transport, no increase of county rates to 'open up' this district. Leave well alone.[76]

In spirited style F.L.D. arranged a petition bearing this legend, against the declared intentions of Cumberland County Council. It attracted the signatures of some 11,000 people who objected, in particular, to five road improvements, submitted in August 1934 to the Government's Commissioner for the Special Area of West Cumberland. These were the following roads, with costs appended: Styhead, £16,500; Wrynose and Hardknott, £12,000 for the four miles which lay in Cumberland; Duddon Bridge, by Buck Barrow and Corney Fell to Waberthwaite, £22,500; Duddon Bridge by the 'Traveller's Rest' and Birker Moor to Eskdale Green, £27,000; and Seatoller by Honister Hause to Buttermere, £6,000.

This 1934 controversy was to be the forerunner and exemplar of many that followed, and merits detailed examination. In its report to the Commissioner the County Council gave four reasons for its suggested 'improvement' of moun-tain roads:

a. the policy would stimulate trade on account of the reduced mileage *b.* it would provide employment whilst the improvement works were in progress

c. it would improve the hotel and apartment trade through bringing visitors into the area

d. it would open up a unique countryside which was, it was argued, 'gradually being forgotten owing to present inaccessibility'.

The honeyed words droned on – 'for bearing in mind the County has some of the finest scenery in Great Britain it would appear very worth while for the Government and the County Council to make this a paying proposition'. The perversity of this peroration won it a place among the classics, yet there was in it a concealed truth – not lucid perhaps in statement, nor too happy in its phrasing, but nevertheless a truth. For by its great beauty the Lake District was paying a high dividend to those who lived and worked in it, for it was inevitable that the District's grandeur and natural simplicity should always attract admirers. But man-handled beauty, it was argued, was a wasting asset and if commercial thinking was the only aim, the 'paying proposition' would slip through careless fingers and be gone.

The scheme to make a £6,000 motor road over Honister Hause was in fact carried through by the County Council on its own initiative, without waiting for any decision or grant from the Commissioner of the Special Area. The Minister of Transport gave an *ad hoc* grant for the Honister road; for doubtless it was felt to deserve State recognition. If the Lake District could not be a National Park, at least Honister, the protest leaflet wryly noted, looked set to be 'a national parking place'.[77]

The National Trust protested in vain, so did the Borrowdale and the Cockermouth Councils, so did every society, local and national concerned in preserving the Lake District. The landowners, hotel-keepers, coach-drivers, rock-climbers, and walkers added their voices to the insistent chorus as the steamrollers rumbled on Honister.

Prior to the works there was already in existence a private toll-road from Seatoller to the Hause, constructed by the Buttermere Slate Company (after the failure of the railway proposals) and up this a private car could pass at any time on payment of a half-crown. For the most part carts using this route turned at the Hause and came back again by the toll-road to Seatoller. There was thus no regular through traffic of cars from Borrowdale to Buttermere. The toll-road could have been purchased by the County Council for £2,000 – 20 times the average annual receipt in tolls. But rather than purchase and re-surface the existing toll-road, which was well graded and little used by walkers, the Council made up, as a second motor road on the Seatoller side the old lane that ran by Hause Gill to the summit, and then continued it as a motor road down to Gatesgarth above Buttermere. Hause Gill became a terror for walkers, and also, by reason of its deceptively steep gradient, very dangerous for cars. The planners, by their perversity, had provided two roads on one side of the pass.

The £27,000 scheme for the road from Ulpha to Eskdale Green, and that for motorizing the Hardknott Pass received no grants from the Commissioner. The first scheme was considered by the Cumbria Highways Committee in 1936 as an independent proposal (to cost £32,000). In the event, the Committee rejected the proposal laid before them, and a quite reasonable resurfacing and easing of the bad points on Birker Moor was carried out. This met with guarded approval because it was felt that there should be good motor access round, and to, the circumference of the district, though not into the inner heart of it, or into any dales that had not been opened up.

The Highways Committee also considered the Commissioner's refusal over Hardknott, and again rejected a scheme for considerable improvement, so that it could be part of a through motor route. The Wrynose-Hardknott route was, and is, an essential route in any itinerary for walking in the Lake District, with views from the top down the green lengths of mid-Eskdale.[78] The proposal to motorize Styhead was dropped after being soundly execrated, and of the proposed through route from Duddon Bridge to Waberthwaite no more was heard. Of the five schemes put to the Commissioner in 1934 by Cumberland the Honister scheme was forced through, that for Birker Moor was carried out with reasoned moderation, and the other three suspended.

The devastation then proposed was in one respect incomplete, for a part of the road system (Newlands Pass) linking Borrowdale and Buttermere with Keswick was in 1934 omitted. Less beautiful than the old lane which delightfully climbed up Hause Gill to Honister, there was a 7 ft grass track climbing over Newlands Hause to Buttermere. Horse-drawn coaches used it in earlier years, as they had used Honister. For a car there was available, between Buttermere and Keswick, the first-class road by Whinlatter. The proposal to increase the Newlands track to 25ft width of tarmac was announced in 1936. It led to urgent protest to the Ministry of Transport, but the walker was driven out to instal the motorist, and the authority of the car was asserted in December 1937 at the same time as a bypass was proposed for Ambleside.[79] Mechanical noise was also becoming more evident and led to protests from the Anti-Noise League. They objected to motor-cycle trialists using mountain tracks, including those near to Hardknott and Wrynose. Aeroplanes had started to fly low over Windermere and motor speed boats skimmed across the surfaces of several lakes.

In addition to the five schemes noted above, the County Council also proposed, wisely enough, a radical improvement of the tortuous coast road (A595) through west Cumberland. The Special Commissioner made no grant, despite the advantages of linking the industries of west Cumberland with Lancashire. But the scheme had the support of the amenity groups because they felt that any proposal to improve the ring-roads round the Lake District eased pressure at the centre and removed the need for cars to use the steep passes.

The width of roads was a crucial issue. In 1925–6 careful work had been done in Borrowdale and Langdale, but the worry was that the ease of access would encourage the Traffic Commissioners to licence motor-buses to ply up and down Borrowdale, and that 'Keswick to Keswick, via Ambleside and Langdale Head' would appear in the bill-of-fare of charabanc and 'bus proprietors. In 1932 the authors of the *Cumbrian Regional Planning Scheme*, Patrick Abercrombie and Sydney Kelly, had noted that the rough and pleasant lane between Seatoller and Seathwaite was 'one of the best examples of those continuations of a main road towards the dale-head. To widen them would not only be extravagant, but would destroy much roadside beauty.'[80] But within two or three years it had become a formal tar-macadam road of 14ft width, driven for a mile and a half into the cul-de-sac towards Styhead.

So far the discussion has in the main concerned the policy of the mid thirties towards the lesser mountain passes and dale roads which run only as far as the confronting barrier of the fells. What was happening to the main through-traffic roads of the Lake District? These were two in number. No passes from east to west penetrated the barrier of the High Street range and this contributed to the seclusion and simplicity of life in its vicinity. The result was that the through routes in the Lake District ran only north and south – from Penrith along Ullswater and over Kirkstone down to Windermere (A592), and from Keswick over Dunmail Raise to Windermere and Kendal (A591). To this absence of a traffic artery from east to west, more than to any other cause, is due the superiority of mountain solitude which the Lake District holds against North Wales. The latter, by the formation of its mountains, gives a natural encouragement to a criss-cross system of main roads.

The Kirkstone road has for the most part kept its simple character and moderate width. As a Road Authority, Westmorland Council had an eye to its wild beauty. The Kirkstone gap, an obvious highway since primitive man roamed there, and about which Wordsworth wrote, 'we find no appanage of human kind', has a modest road with low informal walling, and the road is no scar to the fellside. The road from Keswick to Dunmail Raise to Windermere runs north to south through the geological fault of which the Vale of St John is the north end. In 1931 this important road became the subject of an acrimonious debate.

The Minister of Transport was pressing for a drastic widening and reconstruction of the road, but was opposed by Westmorland County Council. As a result of a conference with the Council and the C.P.R.E. it was agreed that the road was of exceptional character and therefore that a normal maximum width between fences need not be enforced by the Ministry as a condition of a full grant. Very sympathetic treatment was also given by the Westmorland Highways Committee and its officials to the road length south of Rydal village where a 'diverted' footpath runs along the outer side of an avenue of trees. The area remains as it must so long have been, and contains the most beautiful stretch of main road in north-west England.

The road north to Scotland prior to the construction of the motorway (M6) was the A6, known throughout England for the steep exposed gradients of Shap. In snow and frost drivers of lorries frequently resorted to the less exposed A591. It was a wrong use by industrial transport and in 1939, when F.L.D. issued its *A Road Policy for the Lake District*, two radical reconstructions seemed necessary; firstly, the reconstruction of the west-coast road (A595) which remains comparatively snow-free, and secondly a revised alignment of the A6 (a trunk road under the control of the Ministry of Transport) to give it a maximum altitude lower by 300 ft and a less exposed approach to the summit.

Unhappily the 1931 conference concerned only the Westmorland part of the Windermere to Keswick road (A591). Widening in 1935 at a cost of £16,500 between the Thirlmere valley and the summit above Keswick (Ness Brow) produced effects most unsuitable to the district. An excessive carriageway of 30 ft, and an emphatic double verge, part grass, part tarmac footpath, gave an over-all measurement of 40 ft. And a regrettably exact and elaborate system of walling was also erected, with the stones unnaturally squared and patterned, and mechanically accurate battlements. The total effect is still suburban.

The position in the late thirties, which underpins all later problems, projections, improvements, and despoliation was summarized thus by F.L.D.:

a. a policy needed to be formulated between the Ministry, the local highway authorities, the Traffic Commissioners, and where possible the amenity societies

b. the ruling that the Ministry refused construction grants for a lesser over-all width than 40 ft needed to be reversed[81]

c. a list of roads was needed that the local highway authorities undertook not to 'improve'. Such a list would express a considered policy for the Lake District as an undivided whole

d. a check was needed to the increasing and excessive number of touring charabancs using the minor roads in the Lake District.

Finally the F.L.D. road policy booklet urged making the district a National Park, and concluded with apposite words from John Bunyan's *The Pilgrim's Progress*:

'I love to be' says Mercy 'in such places where there is no rattling with coaches, nor rumbling with wheels: methinks here a man may, without much molestation, be thinking of what he is, whence he came, what he has done, and to what the King has called him.'

In 1938 England had just over three million registered motor vehicles. By 1960 the number had grown to more than eight and a half million, and was increasing by about three-quarters of a million every year. At Whitsuntide 1960 the Royal Automobile Club organized traffic counts on the chief roads entering the Lake District. These showed an increase for all traffic of 40 per cent over the previous year. Vehicles crossing the Kirkstone Pass on the Sunday and Monday evenings of the holiday weekend passed the check point at the rate of, respectively, 1,500 and 2,100 an hour – a vehicle every two seconds.

A morbid interest arose in the growing volume of statistics. A Ministry of Transport census taken in five months (March to August) in 1959 showed that in August the average daily total of motor vehicles of all classes passing along the Windermere to Ambleside portion of the A591 had doubled since 1938. The Minister of Transport had envisaged a still more daunting prospect. The seaside of the future, he thought (and perhaps also the countryside, others mused), might become 'nothing more than a huge car park with drainage, water and plug-in telephones for the travelling caravans'.[82] The designation of the Lake District as a National Park in 1951 was also exerting an indirect pressure by the growing amenities that made it an even more attractive place to visit by a wide public which had the means to do so.

It was over 25 years since F.L.D. had issued (in 1939) its pamphlet urging a road policy. In 1961 F.L.D. again stated the problems in a pamphlet. It argued that the result of making provision for more cars by widening and straightening roads was only to attract more cars, so that the authorities' policy was self-defeating. The Lake District needed treatment quite different from that which might well be appropriate to more densely-populated areas. Ownership of a motor-car was becoming the expectation of the majority, and as the Buchanan Report on Traffic in Towns tersely put it

> Regarded in its collective aspect as the 'traffic problem' the motor car is clearly a menace which can spoil our civilisation. We have been appalled by the magnitude of the problem and by the speed with which it is advancing upon us. Unless the greatest care is exercised it will be easily within our ability to ruin this island by the end of the century.[83]

Traffic problems in the Lake District – the words have all too familiar a ring – were further complicated in the late 1950s, by the volume of heavy industrial traffic using the A591 between Kendal and Keswick. In addition it was a road which in the summer carried great numbers of private cars, regular 'bus services (double-decker), and a number of Lake District coach tours. A Ministry of Transport census in August 1959 revealed the following average *daily* totals. For comparison the figures for 1938 and 1954 are also given.

Year	Motor Cycles, etc.	Motor Cars	Buses and Coaches	Lorries and Commercial Vehicles	Total
1938	299	3,145	233	353	4,030
1954	375	3,262	317	711	4,665
1959	635	5,985	295	1,069	7,984

It was established that for considerable portions of the day more than 40 heavy goods vehicles an hour were passing over the road on their way to and from the west Cumberland industrial area.

The concern over the use by lorries was widely felt and in addition the Lake District Planning Board expressed its own concern at the volume of traffic on the A591 and advocated alternative proposals in line with those set out by F.L.D. in its 1961 Road Policy booklet.[84] It was a road which had always provided an alternative route in bad weather to the 1,397 ft summit of Shap on the A6. Hope was also being pinned on the alleviation of problems by the construction of the M6 motorway between Lancaster and Penrith. It was also considered vital that improvements should be made to the west-coast road.

Failure to implement a varied series of corrections and amendments to it would, it was argued, be to subject the very centre of the Lake District and one of the most beautiful National Parks to a damage, which once committed, could never be repaired.

The 1961 F.L.D. pamphlet, near apocalyptic in tone, remains an important policy statement despite much subsequent literature. The crux of the problem was that the Highway Authorities had a virtually unchallengeable say in all that concerned roads in the Lake District, a fatal mistake in the constitution of National Parks.[85] The F.L.D. policy statement attracted considerable support and its aims were also those (with some variations) of the Planning Board, the C.P.R.E., and the Ramblers' Association. It was sent to all Members of Parliament, selected members of the House of Lords, the Ministers of Transport, and Housing and Local Government, the national and local press, local authorities, and to certain university and local libraries. The pamphlet was also discussed by the National Parks Commission.

In the same period of the early sixties, press reports began to circulate revealing that in the representations made by the Cumberland County Planning Officer to the North-West Study Group on Traffic it had been implied that the traffic leaving the motorway for West Cumberland should be routed on the A594. This would pass through Threkeld, alongside Lake Bassenthwaite, with bypasses at Keswick and Cockermouth. It was intended that the A594 from Penrith to Cockermouth should be 'improved' and widened and upgraded to the status of a trunk road, and renumbered the A66.

It was a designation – the A66 – that was to signify the most important confrontation ever to face the amenity groups within the Lake District: 23 miles of the road lay within the National Park. Early in 1965 an article appeared in the *Manchester Guardian* which stated that the Planning Board was undertaking a major investigation into traffic movements, and that it would approach the Planning Officers of the three counties that comprised the Park (Cumberland, Westmorland, Lancashire) about moves that could be taken to modify the A66 scheme.[86] The F.L.D. officers worked hard throughout the year to arrange a meeting of the 20 objecting organizations. This finally took place at Buxton and two of the resolutions passed were of great moment. It was resolved that the Government should be informed that the conference expressed very grave concern at the consequences of a planning system which allowed alterations of such magnitude to a National Park to be made without reference to the planning authority. They were to be urged to bring such matters under planning control.[87] Secondly it was resolved to press the government to commission, without delay, a 'rural Buchanan Report', to look at the problem of traffic in National Parks, with recommendations for easing traffic difficulties, but ensuring that natural beauty remained undisturbed. As early as 1945 John Dower had predicted that the peace and quiet of the countryside, enjoyed by residents and visitors alike, would suffer great damage by 'wholesale widenings, straightenings and flattenings, and from the encouragement they give to ever-heavier and ever-faster traffic'.[88]

The 'A66 campaign' story is a long and involved one and has received very detailed examination elsewhere.[89] Many aspects reflect with great discredit on the Department of the Environment (D.O.E.); for example, Alan F. Holford-Walker, Joint Secretary of the C.P.R.E., observed during the later A66 Inquiry that the Department had made it quite clear that unless it got its way over the A66 improvements there could be no guarantee that funds would be available for any other link route.[90] This was a sharp threat to Cumberland County Council which would thus have had to bear sole financial responsibility for the costs of the A66 works. The upgrading of the A594 to trunk status as the A66 in April 1968 meant that the D.O.E. had become the official highway authority for this stretch of road and was therefore responsible for the financial outlay required.

Meeting followed meeting with a notable absence of useful assurances, but many bland assertions that the D.O.E. was 'keenly aware of the necessity to preserve the amenity of the Lake District'.[91] The Planning Board was also in a delicate position as the Redcliffe-Maud report on local government in England had made little reference to the future of such Boards and left their position unclear. They did not therefore, at such a stage, wish to make forceful objections to the D.O.E. about its road proposals. It was also noted that the Ministry of Transport had included some £2 million in its early 1970s road programme for the construction of a northern bypass at Keswick, part of the A66 scheme.

One of the major problems for people opposing the D.O.E.'s proposals or commitments was that future official moves were kept a closely guarded secret. Only as the extent of the works became apparent was public opinion marshalled, and by then it was really too late. Insufficient information, limited political access (though approaches were made to 40 Members of Parliament), and no formal part in the planning decisions hampered the amenity societies. Modifications, not wholesale change, became the urgently revised battle-cry.

It may be useful at this point to remind the reader what the major proposals were in the A66 scheme:

a. to turn the Penrith–Keswick–Cockermouth road (A66) into a major industrial route to West Cumberland

b. to dual the carriageway along the western shore of Bassenthwaite Lake

c. to construct an entirely new fast road round Keswick, crossing the River Greta, on a 100ft high viaduct and circling the slopes to the north of the town

d. to design a route, with lengths of new road, new bridges, roundabouts, and intersections, to bring fast commercial traffic from the M6 Motorway through the Lake District to industrial west Cumberland.

The objectors set out five points, and an alternative to the proposals:[92]

a. a major industrial highway should not be brought through Britain's premier National Park

b. the vast engineering works involved were completely out of keeping with the small intimate scale of the Lake District

c. the route round Keswick, with its viaduct and motorway type interchange would alter the whole character of the fine unspoilt hill background to the town

d. fast dual carriageways along the western shores of Bassenthwaite Lake would destroy its natural setting, especially as part of the road would be built on embankment out into the lake

e. there was a good valid alternative route for industrial traffic to west Cumberland, viz., the A595 and an improved B5305 from the M6, outside the National Park

f. lastly it was hoped that Keswick's traffic problems could be relieved by a more modest northern bypass of the town.

There was a growing unease in the amenity group committees that the intended construction of a new plant in West Cumberland for the manufacture of buses by a new company formed by British Leyland and the National Bus Company had much to do with the campaign for improved access to the M6.

Running concurrently with the A66 problem was the proposal set out in February 1970 to improve access to Barrow-in-Furness, a remote industrial town, by a Barrow–Arnside link road connected with the M6 and A6.[93] Amenity groups usually feel an instinctive antipathy to any proposal for a new highway, but it was recognized that the best reaction was one based on logical argument, carefully researched.

At the edge of the National Park a fierce battle was about to start on the ancillary problems associated with the new Kendal link to the M6 which on the proposed 'Route C' would take the 24ft carriageways through the northern end of Levens Park.

Levens Park, with its great 2,000yd-long oak avenue set out in the late 17th century by Guillaume Beaumont, Colonel Graham's French gardener, is a unique form of landscaping. It was altered, alas, by the coming of the turnpike road in the 1750s, now the busy A6. That road, at Levens Bridge, did however skirt the house and the formal topiary gardens, even if it isolated the Park. The route of the proposed new link road was so calculated that if carried out it would destroy one of the earliest park layouts in the country.

The owners of Levens, Robin and Annette Bagot, led a spirited campaign, recognizing that an alternative route was possible, given some common-sense and a will to preserve a unique stretch of English parkland. The point of Beaumont's avenue was the view it focused over the River Kent. A major highway on a massive concrete bridge, 310 ft long, is not an easy item to accommodate. To move it about 100 yd north would at least preserve the unity of the Park, the avenue, and the view across the gorge.[94] Reason did prevail here and the visitor to Levens may still walk in the Park, described in 1780 by Thomas West in his *Guide to the Lakes* as 'the sweetest spot that fancy can imagine'. The herd of black fallow deer grazes on undisturbed.

The Barrow road proposals went to public inquiry and with evidence from Geoffrey Berry and technical aspects covered by Hugh Wilson and J. Lewis

Womersley (architects and town planners) a very convincing case was made.[95] In January 1973 the Secretary of State for the Environment, Geoffrey Rippon, announced that the draft orders had been withdrawn, and 'there is no equivocation about possibly proceeding later if no barrage is built'.[96] It was a victory for the 'amenity argument', and a recognition of the potential impact of environmental damage in areas of sensitive landscape values.

In the early seventies support was mobilized for continuing the campaign against the A66's route and scale. In the first months of 1972 F.L.D. published a careful and well-argued traffic management report written by Wilson and Womersley.[97] This supported the Society's arguments against road alterations damaging the environment. Its publication was timed appropriately to precede the opening of the public inquiry on the A66. It was soon evident that the issues to be debated were more than usually complicated.

The campaign continued at levels of national significance. Members of Parliament were bombarded with letters and information, and every opportunity was seized to state the alternatives to the proposed route. Correspondence flowed in to F.L.D. from all over the British Isles as well as from individuals in America, Canada, and even Hong Kong. Ten thousand copies of the protest leaflet were circulated initially, followed by a further 30,000 to members of the Ramblers' Association. The lobby was strengthened when the Countryside Commission, a statutory body, confirmed that its view was that a less objectionable route could be found to the north of Skiddaw (B5305), and outside the National Park.[98] The inquiry was announced for 25 January 1972 at Penrith, with Sir Robert Scott as the presiding Inspector.

The Countryside Commission and the Lake District Planning Board with the sympathetic support of F.L.D. and many other amenity bodies supported the opposition. The Countryside Commission briefed expert counsel and witnesses, a vital prerequisite if any significant inroads were to be made on the industrial and social factors involved. At stake was the unique quality of the scenery with which the proposed road-works would interfere, with destructive effect. The business lobby which extolled the benefits of the A66 was represented by the Cumberland Development Council chaired by Sir Frank (later Lord) Schon. It became the most outspoken of the pro-A66 groups, and argued that improved roads were necessary not only for industrial west Cumberland but also for tourists and leisure-motorists. Its Secretary, Arthur Eaton, described the environmentalists' objections as a 'misguided exercise of a minority group'.[99]

It was to be expected that the arguments would increase in ferocity as the inquiry date drew nearer. No one denied that industry had declined, and that efforts to regenerate the area had met with many difficulties. But it was held by many that a better road across the Lake District to west Cumberland would be the best hope for industrial recovery.[100]

A general feeling had started to grow that the inquiry would be something of a farce, set in motion to encourage continued belief in the democratic process. Comments were also made about some form of government-business liaison operating behind the scenes. It was soon confirmed that British Leyland was reluctant to establish a £9 million bus plant near the coast without improved access to the M6. Michael McCarthy has noted comments by Lord Stokes to 'the new road improvements' made some 15 months before the inquiry took place.[101] There seemed little doubt that the proposals would go through, for Prime Minister Harold Wilson had stated his own belief in the necessity of improving this road, prefaced by the phrase 'after strong pressure from me'.[102] But assumptions, suspicions, and conclusions remain for the most part unconfirmed, and those interested must read 'between the lines' of the lengthy Inquiry Report.

The A66 proposals had wide implications for the National Park. The alternative route via Sebergham was costed at £13.92 million, a little over £1 million more than the one proposed – a very small price to pay for the preservation of a National Park – and other factors reduced even this margin.[103] The Simpson-Zetter report commissioned by the Countryside Commission and the Lake District Special Planning Board, and the Traffic Management study issued by F.L.D. were, of course, well criticized.[104] F.L.D. was not happy either with Simpson and Zetter's conclusions, although their report contained valuable engineering information. However, the amenity bodies needed to counter critics who saw amenity in terms of what it offered the motorist rather than the traditional users of the Lake District. It was 'access' encouragement of the wrong kind. Whilst nationally much was known about the likely impact of the A66, the residents of Keswick seemed unaware, even in broad outline, of what was mooted to circle their town.

The Inquiry Inspector delivered his report, and the Secretary of State, Geoffrey Rippon, announced on 22 December 1972 his decision to pass the A66 proposals. The Inspector had said a great deal, but one paragraph summarized his views.

> Access must remain one of the principal purposes of the Park because it is the prerequisite to public enjoyment. Important as conservation is, the Park is not a nature reserve from which visitors are to be excluded. I do not accept that all other considerations must be subordinated to it.[105]

The Secretary of State was thus prepared to see damage done to the National Park landscape – grave and irremediable damage – in order that unlimited numbers of lorries and cars should be able to travel at high speed through the National Park, destroying the very entity most people come to see and enjoy. The primary purpose of National Parks had been betrayed, the views of the statutory bodies set aside, and the overall planning of the Lake District in traffic terms ignored.[106] The Inspector was criticized for not weighing all the evidence impartially, and the Liberal spokesman on the Environment, Hugh Heywood, said that 'approval for the A66 "improvements" meant . . . a sombre outlook for the National Park'.[107]

The decision was followed by a period in which debate and comment were punctuated by long intervals of vague evasion, and the ineffectual efforts of a working-party, from which F.L.D. was excluded. The outcome was a decision not to set up any organization to study the Lake District's traffic problems until after local government reorganization in April 1974. The lobbying went on unabated, with a protest rally on the slopes of Latrigg overlooking much of the A66 route. The day after the event, which took place on 14 October 1973, the *Daily Telegraph* summed up in firm tones:

> This is a crime, make no mistake. It is a matter of commercial greed against humanity: of God and Mammon. You may think a road through the Lake District is a trivial matter to demonstrate about compared with other things that are going on in the world. Then you are wrong.

F.L.D. for its part took note of the criticisms of its seeming pungency and inflexibility: it is easy to over-react, but when areas of great natural beauty are involved, some emotive issues are bound to be interspersed with the essential technical information. But all amenity groups try to adopt an over-all view of the problem, even if they succeed only partially. The result without their intervention is, however, frequently disastrous, and certainly little understood by the general public whose lives are so affected by what authorities decide for them.

An example of this was the proposed bypass for Ambleside, first suggested in December 1937 and raised again in 1970 and 1979. All the old well-tried reasons for it came forward, particularly the high August traffic figures, to suggest a continuing pattern which in fact existed for a short period only. The route suggested for the bypass, across the Rothay meadows with the graceful spired church in the background, would have violated a stretch of delightful Wordsworthian scenery. Regrettably the Lake District Planning Board accepted the scheme in principle.

A public inquiry was held in October 1973 at which it was pointed out that the standard design of the road necessitated continuous embankment or cutting along its entire length, resulting in a construction completely different from any existing road in the area. Furthermore, the traffic projections were wildly optimistic at a period when, increasingly, shortages and price rises of oil were beginning to take effect on motoring. It was also contended that whatever these effects on private motoring, heavier traffic should be excluded from using the A591 through Ambleside itself.[108] Once again, the lack of a co-ordinated policy for Lake District traffic was compounding the issue. After a delay of 18 months the Secretary of State for the Environment refused permission for the bypass due to its potentially serious impact and detrimental effects on the environment of the area and on property in the vicinity of the route.[109]

At the same time recognition was given to the serious traffic problems and congestion in Ambleside and a one-way system of traffic management was suggested and introduced for a trial period. This had been resisted by local shopkeepers as damaging to their trade – but would it not have been worse with a bypass? The fact has to be faced that whatever is done, even if in the future a bypass is built, Ambleside will never be peaceful. Traffic will continue to fill the main streets in high summer and holidays. For many people, the little towns with their gift shops are the objects of their visits to the Lake District. Bypasses at Carlisle, Kendal, and Keswick have not produced peaceful towns.

Finally, there was another proposed bypass likely to have similarly devastating impact on its area – the bypass for Staveley, five miles from Kendal on the A591 to Windermere. Westmorland County Council had sought consent from the Lake District Planning Board for the construction of a 24ft dual carriageway to bypass Staveley village on its southern side. Permission was refused on the grounds that 'the construction of a high-speed dual carriageway road would be out of character with the Lake District National Park and contrary to the Board's formulated policy' and that the A591 'should be predominantly a single carriageway road'.[110] The refusal led again to a public inquiry in January 1974 – and to a memorable phrase from an American member of F.L.D.: 'don't let them Californicate the Lake District'.

The bypass was also refused by the Secretary of State in September 1974. No one disputed the need for it, but the proposal had been for a grandiose road, with dual carriageways, and was, not surprisingly, ruled out as unnecessarily large and damaging. A single-carriageway bypass would undoubtedly have obtained immediate approval, and the work would now have been completed. But the Highway Authority, thwarted by the refusal of its scheme, abandoned any early intention of getting on with what must be regarded as an urgent necessity. Perhaps every highway engineer should have over his desk a poker-work legend of these words set out in John Dower's seminal report of 1945:

> It does not follow that motorists have any proper claim for the endless widening and improvement of . . . roads to enable them to travel everywhere at high speeds, regardless of 'the view' and without risk of congestion, however many of them may take simultaneously the same Sunday outing.

V *The Carriage Trade*

The views of mountain and lake scenery commanded from the
windows are unsurpassed by any in the district. Open and Close
Carriages, Cars, and Post-Horses always in readiness.

Advertisement for Rigg's Windermere Hotel in Harriet Martineau
Guide to Windermere (*c.* 1857)

Miss Harriet Martineau issued the second (undated) edition of her *Guide to
Windermere* in the late 1850s. She owned in it that the village was so changed
by tourists brought by the railway Wordsworth had derided that her new
guidebook was necessary 'as there is much more to point out than there used
to be'. Also the fulsome advertisements at the end of her little book included
not only many more for hotels, but one which informed the curious that David
Armstrong 'since last season' had so improved his Museum and Fancy Repo-
sitory at Bowness that the collection now comprised not only 'British Birds,
Reptiles and Quadrupeds' but also 'Roman and other Coins, and a great variety
of miscellaneous interesting curiosities'. They were the sort of amiable delights,
natural and man-made, that early tourists sought out eagerly, and which, in
addition to natural wonders, their modern counterparts still seek.[111]

Admittedly as Edmund W. Hodge has pointed out, a perfectly preserved
Lake District might 'be really rather dull for the holiday-maker who did not
happen to be a poet-mystic on the run from revolution, love, or the life of his
time'.[112] What should be accepted by any serious thinker about life and leisure
in the Lake District is that it *should* be visited – in great numbers if needs be –
but that careful measures are necessary to contain the influx and to avoid
unthinking sterility. It is easy to assume that the area should be a national
'amusement park' catering for every recreational activity. But the 1949 Act
defined the National Parks as tracts of country that should be preserved for the
enjoyment of the public because of their natural beauty, and the opportunities
they afford for open-air recreation and the study of nature. It has been stated
that naturally, and not unreasonably, 'activities which conflict with the funda-
mental purpose for which national parks were established should not be
encouraged'.[113]

Firstly 'users' of the National Park may be divided into those who were born
and bred within its confines, and those who have come in and settled because
they like it. Secondly, there are the people who visit it regularly, winter and
summer, because they find something they want or really need. Thirdly, the
Lake District is a holiday area for tourists, and there is great provision for
weekenders and day-trippers. Finally there are the discerning, or brisk crowds
of foreign visitors who with pennants flying and maps at the ready are com-

paring what they see with Switzerland, Germany, France, or Sweden.[114] Some of them come in strange conveyances.

Miss Martineau in her guide to the Lake District assumed that the traveller of her day would come by train to Oxenholme junction, and thence by train through Kendal to Windermere. While many, particularly groups of walkers and climbers, still use this route, the vast majority come by car and, in increasing numbers since the late 1940s, with a caravan or something even bigger towed behind. When the Lake District Planning Board came into existence in 1951 it recognized that it had a responsibility to see that sites for caravanning and camping were available. But it was also realized that such sites, with sanitary and other amenities, had to be located well down the dales, where they could be sufficiently screened and command the necessary water supplies and proper drainage.[115] At this time, and subject to these provisions, new sites were to be allowed as they added to the total accommodation available, and enabled more people to visit the Lake District.

In 1951 there were 11,000 members of the Caravan Club of Great Britain; by 1960 44,000; and by 1968 over 95,000. Membership of the Camping Club grew similarly from nearly 14,000 in 1950 to 120,000 by 1968.[116] It was a pressure at variance with a number of other interests which had been expressed clearly in the years around the setting up of National Parks. The Country Landowners' Association took the view that the maintenance of agriculture and forestry were important, and the Chartered Surveyors and the Land Agents Society in a joint memorandum stressed the importance of farming: 'the permanent interests of those who live and work in any of these areas should in common justice be given precedence over the transitory interests of the visitors'.[117]

As in towns the question of car parking became dominant. The Lake District car parks in the main are small, tree-screened, and carefully sited. There are exceptions, the most notable of which is undoubtedly the vast exposed car park on the edge of Hawkshead. The parking problem has become more acute as visitors increase, and consideration has been given to the possibility of providing large car parks from which mini-buses would operate, as in Derbyshire's Goyt Valley scheme. A problem, however, is that the pressure exists mainly at holiday periods – during the months of July and August, at Easter, Whitsuntide, and Summer Bank Holiday weekends, and on fine Sundays from early spring to late autumn.[118] It is difficult to justify a large area of hard-core, little used at other times. However well-screened, it is an intrusion into the landscape.

Such 'intrusion' had always been a basic problem with the caravan, and the Planning Board, busy in providing its own carefully placed sites, had set down certain criteria to be observed. These had been forced upon the Board by the rapid increase in numbers, resulting in over-crowding on existing sites, the spread of these sites outside permitted areas, the use of lay-bys and disused sections of road for overnight stays, the creation of unauthorized sites for both camping and caravanning, and trespass onto neighbouring land. Cumberland Countryside Conference discussed these matters in 1971–2,[119] and the Board also revised its policy in 1974.[120] One welcome feature was the establishment of the Board's Caravan Advisory Service to give information on where pitches are likely to be available, and this is now run in conjunction with the Cumbria Tourist Board. It has been outstandingly successful, and has done a great deal to discourage the motorist who points his car bonnet towards the north-west under the impression that no pitch need be booked in advance.

As well as caravans on tow, the A591 north to Ambleside is busy in the spring with cars towing boats, some of which are being returned to moorings for the season. In addition, throughout the summer many boat-owners like to trail their craft to and from a lake to avoid the high cost of permanent marina moorings. Sailing has always been an attractive feature of life on lakes like Windermere, and practised there since the important regattas of the 1860s.[121] Coniston Water, on the other hand, was increasingly used for speed-boat trials and attempts on the water-speed record. There were no legal measures to control the latter, and Short Brothers' establishment of a seaplane factory at Calgarth on the shores of Windermere for the Ministry of Defence during the Second World War allowed, without risk of stoppage, the throaty roar of marine engines. Control of the use of lake surfaces was needed as recreational activities extended. The growing interest in powered boats and water-skiing started to attract attention from the Planning Board, acting under the powers given to it by Section 13 of the Countryside Act 1968. This allowed it to make by-laws for the prohibition or restriction of traffic of any description on lakes and tarns in the National Park.

In a study such as this, many paragraphs seem to be devoted inevitably to describing a recreational use and then the immediate steps taken to reduce or stop its effects. Motor-boating, and in particular fast motor-boating, and water-skiing came early into this category. Firstly the Planning Board thought it desirable to prohibit the use of motorized craft on 20 lakes and tarns, and by-laws to effect this were approved by the Home Secretary in March 1975.[122] The Planning Board decided to make by-laws to control the speed of motorized craft on Derwent Water, Ullswater, and Coniston Water. This led to a public inquiry at Ambleside in the summer of 1976, starting on 2 August and lasting into October. The Planning Board based its case on a number of varied factors, including the damage to the area from noise and rapid movement on the lakes; the disturbance caused by a relatively small number of people whose requirements could be met elsewhere; the annoyance and danger for other lake-users by speed boats and skiers; and the incompatability of the activities within an area visited by people who sought a natural environment. The Planning Board was supported by the Countryside Commission, the National Trust, F.L.D., C.P.R.E., Cumbria Naturalists' Trust, Youth Hostels Association, Durham County Council, the Forestry Commission, and many other bodies and individuals.

The inquiry accepted that the great majority of the British Water Ski Federation members, and the clubs associated with them, were considerate and observed existing rules, but it was a fact, produced in evidence, that only one-sixth of skiers were members of the clubs. A great deal of evidence was submitted about the bad behaviour of skiers who were usually unattached to any organization. Compulsory membership of clubs was impossible because the three lakes were highways from which the public could not be excluded. Control over the vast majority through club procedures was therefore not feasible.

Some problems arose during the period of the inquiry from comments made by the Minister for Sport, Dennis Howell, on a visit to the Lake District. He had suggested that the only objection to water-skiing was the noise made by power boats, and that could be controlled and dealt with. Noise by-laws in fact already existed, but there had never been a prosecution under them as they were extremely difficult to enforce. In any case the inquiry, which had already been under way for many weeks, had shown that there were many other issues to be considered and debated. One concerned the amount of space used by a power boat and water-skier. If a power boat and skier are travelling at 30 m.p.h., they are not using 10 times as much as a rowing boat going at 3 m.p.h., but 20 times as much, and with the greater speed the power boat spreads its noise over large areas of a lake in a short time.[123]

In the meantime the Special Planning Board looked again at its controls over powered craft on Windermere and decided to strengthen its position. It proposed by-laws to require the registration of all powered craft of whatever engine size, including all craft with outboard engines. This would involve payment of a licence fee and the display of identification numbers. Existing by-laws already required two persons to be in any boat towing a water-skier and imposed speed limits in Bowness Bay and at Waterhead and Lakeside – areas which are exceptionally busy during the summer and autumn months.

Early in 1978 the Home Secretary announced his decision in favour of the by-laws to limit the speed of power boats to 10 miles an hour on Derwent Water, Coniston Water and Ullswater. The by-laws for the first two lakes are now in operation. On Ullswater it is expected that similar by-laws will be confirmed by 1983, thus giving the power-boat-owners and water-skiers time to find other places for their sport. The Inspector (M. Burke-Gaffney) established from the evidence put before him six principles, as follows:

a. The national interest in the Lake District Park must be recognized and given effect to

b. When the twin purposes (conservation and enjoyment) of the Lake District National Park conflict, the main emphasis must be on attempting to reconcile the conflict

c. When the conflict between the two purposes is irreconcilable, priority must be given to the conservation of natural beauty

d. Noisy pursuits, except in some locations and in some degree, or pending transfer elsewhere, are usually out of place in a National Park, and, subject to limited exceptions, provision should not be made for them

e. The problem of fast power-boating on the three Lakes must be looked at in the context of the Lake District National Park as a whole

f. The object of the by-laws is to impose speed limits on vessels exercising a public right to navigate on the three Lakes.

The Inspector had come to the conclusion that in the light of previous case-history there was a public right to navigate on the three Lakes, and on Windermere. Hence zoning schemes which set off parts of the lakes for specific purposes, either by time or space, were ruled out. This and other conclusions showed a formidable written and vocal support for the preservation of peace and tranquillity. The principles led inexorably to the conclusion that generally speaking fast power-boating was incompatible with the National Park concept. Finally, the by-law requiring registration of all power boats using Windermere was confirmed by the Home Secretary and came into force on 1 December 1978.[124] Taken with the *Windermere Recreation Survey* which a steering committee of National Park and South Lakeland District Council staff prepared in 1977, a basis for better recreational use of England's largest lake seems possible. It is rarely short of visitors to try it out.

Much of the Lake District, fortunately, is still the preserve of the climber and walker, but even the paths they tread are continually threatened. Despite there having been an interest in Lake District footpaths from the late 19th century, it was not until the National Parks Act 1949 that it became a duty to make an official survey of all public rights of way. The Ramblers' Association pointed out in 1971 that paths were often ploughed up, closed, or diverted, and that walkers were frequently excluded from wild and lonely places.[125] The Cumbria Footpath Review when announced met with over 300 objections to its detailed proposals; the arguments are not likely to be resolved until the end of 1980.

There is also a need to consider sympathetically other recreations such as snow-skiing, which is carried on in certain areas. Vehicular access is usually necessary, and the Lake District Ski Club is one of the societies whose activities at Raise and elsewhere merit this consideration. A permanent drag tow and hut have been established near 'Savage's Gully' on Raise, and temporary snow-fencing erected to increase the drift and the length of time the snow lies.

Stretches of land where access is restricted are those surrounding reservoirs used for water extraction. When Manchester Corporation was given permission to abstract water from Ullswater and Windermere in 1966, the Minister stated that he would require an undertaking that the Corporation, in conjunction with the Lake District Planning Board, would prepare a detailed programme for allowing further public access to Haweswater and adjoining land. This programme was submitted in March 1968, and with minor modifications it incorporated the proposals put forward in 1965 by the Planning Board.

In September 1973, a meeting of members of Manchester Corporation and the Cumberland River Authority discussed proposals for allowing access to water-gathering grounds and decided to submit them to further review to ensure that they complied with the statutory duty to provide recreational facilities under the Water Act 1973. It was agreed to set up a working party, as the enlargement of Haweswater was not recommended for implementation until 1992. There was therefore a period of at least 12 uninterrupted years for the enjoyment of any additional recreational facilities with the reservoir at present levels. The working party's report was issued in 1974[126] and considered by the Lake District Special Planning Board during that year.[127]

The Board did not however agree to the provision of facilities for various recreational pursuits on an intended site between the dam and Measand Beck. These had included a club house, launching arrangements for sailing, provision for angling, a car park, a picnic area, toilets, and an information unit. There was also opposition to a camp site at Burnbanks, and the development of fishing from shore and boat. And the Board did not consent to the use of the reservoir by motor boats, and had reservations about the establishment of a pony-trekking centre. A proposal to introduce water-skiing to the Wet Sleddale reservoir was again not acceptable to the Board, but the spirit of intended co-operation was welcomed, as it was with the different case of the Forestry Commission's own proposals for visitors in Ennerdale. It was feared that they would have damaging effect on the areas of wilderness.

At Ennerdale the Forestry Commission suggested opening the forests to more people and the provision of various facilities. But it had to be decided how many people could be absorbed into the area without harming the environment. In general the Board's view was that more people could be absorbed, but that the siting of facilities needed careful thought. Bleach Green on the western approach to the lake was seen as a suitable centre for car visitors, picnickers, and campers. Bowness Point on the northern shore should be the place at which those who wished to penetrate on foot further into the valley left their cars. The Forestry Commission set out some 16 miles of forest walk – the Nine Becks walk and the Smithy Beck Forest Trail, the former linking some of the most attractive forest scenery where streams tumble magnificently down to the River Liza. The Forestry Commission says that after heavy rain this walk is without equal.[128]

One of the most attractive walks for casual visitors not equipped for the high fells is the Claife shore walk on the western bank of Windermere. A nature trail leaflet issued by the National Trust and the Freshwater Biological Association (which has been located since 1950 at Ferry Nab, halfway along the Lake), describes a walk on which it is possible to see robins, wrens, goldcrests, magpies, greenfinches, blackbirds, perhaps even roe and red deer, red squirrels, and rabbits. Other nature trails and woodland walks have been created at Thirlmere, in Grizedale Forest, at Brantwood, Ambleside, and Silverdale, and with explanatory leaflets these are among the best ways of learning about the attractive aspects of Lake District natural history.

Attempts have been made for many years to provide programmes of outdoor pursuits. Two of the most successful are those for young people at Brathay, and the work carried out at Brockhole. Brathay was founded by the late Francis Scott in the 18th-century mansion of that name which he acquired from the Redmayne family in 1939. It has developed over some 30 years into an important centre for field studies, explorations, biology and geography courses, with an element of leadership, survival, and 'outward bound' in its varied make-up.

Attractive buildings at Brathay (to designs by Robert Gilchrist) are good examples of modern structures integrated into a National Park landscape.[129]

In 1968 the Planning Board decided to develop Brockhole, about halfway between Windermere and Ambleside, as the first National Park Centre in Britain. The Treasury authorized the National Parks Commission to contribute 80 per cent of the cost of developing and maintaining the Centre. Since that time, under the leadership of its Director John Nettleton, Brockhole has played an important part in exhibiting and depicting, on sound educational lines, the varied aspects of life in the National Park. With its lecture theatres, café, bookstall, exhibitions, and its well-tended gardens on the shores of Windermere, it is one of the most imaginative, informative ventures in this country's National Parks.

Brockhole also acts as the 'flagship' of an extensive National Park Information Service, imaginatively led by Barry Tullett, with its headquarters at Windermere. The Board's Information Centre in Bowness was opened on 1 June 1974 and houses both display and enquiry facilities as well as a small lecture theatre. It proved popular from the start, with 130,000 visitors between opening and the end of the first season. With four mobile units and five visitors' centres at Bowness, Hawkshead, Seatoller, Ambleside, and Keswick, useful programmes of lectures and guided walks, and regular weather and caravan site information are provided to supplement the Brockhole service.

Such activities, important as they are, do not however, touch many thousands of visitors to the Lake District who wander aimlessly and avoid 'instruction'. Two serious problems that arise from the considerable number of visitors are the erosion of paths and grass verges,[130] and walkers and climbers attempting terrain too difficult, without adequate clothing and footwear. Some of the worst examples of the former problem have been alleviated by two phases of an 'Upland Management Experiment',[131] which has led to the establishment of an 'Upland Management Service'. Success has been achieved by maintaining a close connection with farmers, who suggest many of the tasks to be undertaken. These include repairing damage caused by visitors, directly or indirectly, to walls, fences, and stiles, and improving and signing low-level footpaths, constructing footbridges, (as at Thorneythwaite, Borrowdale), and providing footpath diversions away from vulnerable farmland and lambing pastures.

Of the difficulties caused by long-stay visitors, some result from the ownership of second houses in the National Park. This keeps market prices high, and prevents local people competing for either new or existing houses. It encourages young people to leave the area, and combined with the loss of jobs in the typical rural industries, has resulted in a population decline, and a change in age structure. The Special Planning Board's policy of pursuing every possibility to ensure that in the future any new houses anywhere in the National Park will be for local use has led to difficulties and misunderstandings. But whatever the outcome in statistical terms, it is clear that despite Wordsworth's discouragement in the 19th century, and many desirable restrictions in the 20th, visitors will continue to come, and some will stay, bringing employment to many, and causing wrath and indignation to as many more.

VI   *Light to Work By*

When the miner has penetrated into the earth a distance of fifteen or
twenty fathoms, either vertically or horizontally, the supply of fresh
air fails; his candle refuses to burn.

John Postlethwaite *Mines and Mining in the Lake District* (1877)

It became obvious at the turn of the present century that the prosperity and
well-being of life in the countryside was bound up with the spread of rural
electrification. No mine or quarry, no farmhouse, and later, no milking machine
or television set could work effectively without it. Chugging generators, efficient
as they might be, were limited in output and expensive to obtain and keep in
order.

As John Postlethwaite noted in the book from which the chapter-head quo-
tation comes, mining in the early days was a dirty and dangerous undertaking.
Noxious gases were frequently liberated from cavities in the rock which had a
very injurious effect upon the miner's respiratory organs. These, combined with
the mineral dust he inhaled, in a period before the safeguarding Acts of Parliament had enforced effective measures to combat it, produced in him the seeds
of disease and premature old age.

Mining has taken place in the Lake District since Roman times, but its most
interesting phase came in the late 16th century when the Company of Mines
Royal worked for copper in the valley of the Red Dell Beck at Coniston. In the
17th century English miners were joined by immigrant miners from Germany
and Austria.[132] Gunpowder works were set up in the 1760s in Westmorland,
lead was mined at Greenside, near Lake Ullswater, and at Alston, and the
plumbago mine in Borrowdale gave rise to pencil manufacture at Keswick.
Wolframite, various ores of copper, iron pyrites and barytes, limestone, granite,
slate, and igneous rock have also been worked.[133] The most extensive and best-
known of Lake District quarries are those at Honister, Kirkstone, Elterwater,
and Coniston, which have provided slate for roofing and building purposes
from the mid 18th century onwards.

In 1864 Mrs E. Lynn Linton provided a graphic description of the Honister
quarrymen in which she noted:

> this slate quarrying is awful to look at; both in the giddy height at which
> men work, and in the terrible journeys which they make when bringing
> down the slate in their sleds . . . it is a terrible trade, and the men
> employed in it look wan and worn, as if they were all consumptive or had
> heart disease.[134]

While conditions improved, the great spoil-heaps were steadily added to. In

1928 the total output of slate in Cumberland was 2,478 tons, an increase of 682 tons on the previous year, but less than half the output of 20 years earlier.[135] In 1978 eight slate quarries were at work, and the Kirkstone Green Slate Quarry owners at Skelwith Bridge have also opened a gift shop, café, and showroom for their products, which are busy, winter and summer, with tourists. It is an attractive spot above the dramatic whirling waters of the Brathay, and car-parking is already inadequate for even fine winter weekends.

In the early 1930s concern about the mineral dumps was becoming focused. F. L. D. was disturbed about those at Greenside, Thornthwaite, Borrowdale, in the Duddon Valley above Ulpha, and at Kirkstone and Hartsop wood.[136] In addition, considerable concern was being expressed about the discoloured state of Glenridding Beck, caused by discharge from the Greenside Lead Mine. A year or two before F. L. D. became involved it was noted, in 1932, that gravel washed down the beck was forming a wide delta at the head of Ullswater.[137]

Problems of this kind continue, increase in effect, and are only alleviated if concerted action is made and accepted. By August 1938 the Basinghall Mining Syndicate, which worked Greenside, had to be informed that the pollution of Ullswater was serious. Analysis was undertaken on several occasions, and a misleading article on the situation in *The Times* had to be corrected in that no improvement was to be seen in the beck and lake as stated.[138] The National Trust was considering taking joint legal action with Ullswater Hotel Ltd to obtain an injunction against the Mining Syndicate, but this was finally set aside despite little improvement. Daily sampling of the water continued, meetings were held locally and in London, but by July 1941 it was agreed that 'the negotiations of the past two years now seemed to have produced no benefit'.[139]

At a conference in London on 3 November 1941 between the National Trust, the Syndicate, and the Attorney-General, it was stated that a fiat would be delayed until the parties had negotiated further, with a view to making a settlement satisfactory to both. The Syndicate claimed that for the 12 weeks up to the beginning of November the average amount of solids going down the beck per week was 2½ tons. In the negotiations that the Attorney-General had requested the Syndicate countered the National Trust's request to them for effective control of the mine effluent by asking for a quantitative definition of the degree of pollution that would be allowed. This was refused, the negotiations were held to have failed, and a writ was finally issued against the Syndicate. There were soon fears that because the mine was producing a valuable product, the Ministry of Supply, under its wartime powers, would make the nuisance non-actionable. The daily samples of beck-water had shown that the amount of solids going down to the lake during the first three months of 1942 had varied from 2½ tons per week (a fairly good figure) to more than 7 tons per week. This far exceeded the Royal Commission on Sewage Disposal's recommendation for lead workings, of 6 parts solid in 100,000 parts of water, probably giving a total of some 12 hundredweight a week.

As expected the Ministry of Supply did issue an order permitting continued lead mining 'notwithstanding that a nuisance may be caused thereby', subject however to two conditions: a) the pumping of the effluent to the tailings dam, and its clarification *there* before discharge to the beck, and b) reasonable precautions against any break-up of the dump. It was a stalemate situation; it dragged on, and was not resolved until, with the vein worked out, the mine closed in 1962. One of its buildings is now the Greenside Youth Hostel. In its heyday the mine had been a pioneer in the use of electrical power – electric haulage being introduced in 1891, and an electric locomotive in 1893.[140]

One of the main problems which faced the Honister slate quarrymen by contrast was transport. The slate had to be sent over 15 miles to be loaded at Ravenglass, and Mrs Linton records how it was brought down the steep hillside by the men on 'sleds', carrying a quarter of a ton of slate each time.[141] Railways provided a considerable stimulus to quarrying, and the opening in 1859 of the Coniston branch of the Furness Railway assisted the slate workings enterprise. But it was an inevitable consequence of the steady extraction that a high proportion of waste found its way to the towering spoil-heaps.

At Honister there are now vast open workings, which, with the associated roads and tips, can be seen from an extensive area. From as far away as Greenup Edge it now appears that the skyline of Honister Crag is being assailed. The prominent situation of Bursting Stones Quarry on the southern face of Coniston Old Man has given frequent cause for complaint. The Kirkstone Quarry has also been described as a shattering example of a quarry in the wrong place. The large open cavities and spoil-heaps on the exposed mountainside have grown dramatically in recent years. It is alarming to contemplate what this famous pass will look like in a few years' time if extraction goes on at this or, more probably, at an increasing rate. The streams from all these quarries are at times polluted, and in particular the Gatesgarth Beck is often an obtrusive milky white from the head of Honister Pass for some two miles, and appears to be devoid of life.

The authors recognize that quarrying is a traditional Lake District industry and that there are difficulties in enforcing planning conditions imposed many years ago. These may, in any case, now be inadequate to cope with present-day operating requirements. Kirkstone Quarry is an example of this. It was originally one of many small disused slate quarries scattered about the Lake District which had largely merged into the landscape by weathering action and the passage of time. The quarry was reopened in a very small way in 1950. It was proposed to concentrate on the large amount of rock on the quarry bed, and working on the quarry face was expected to be insignificant. But the business expanded, and an application extensions was made in 1963. Because of the difficulty of assessing the effects on the landscape the permission was limited to 15 years. However this did not cover the full period of the applicant's lease, and on appeal, and following a public inquiry, the Minister extended the approval period to 25 years.

The large percentage of waste – as much as 95 per cent in some cases – is one of the main problems, as it is virtually impossible to assimilate waste stone into the landscape. To remove it would be expensive and put a burden of heavy lorries on steep, narrow, twisting roads. As green slate is only found in the Lake District the Special Planning Board recognized its special importance. Its traditional use as a building material had long been appreciated, but since the early 1960s it has become fashionable for architectural use. This has increased the scale of working, the Planning Board having little control over this with existing planning law.[142]

The Planning Board accepted the continued working of existing slate quarries because they provide local employment, but any new ones or large extensions would need to be assessed according to their location and effect on the landscape. Quarry operators were also being urged to examine less wasteful methods of extraction and processing, to minimize the quantity of waste produced, or find suitable uses for the material. It was suggested that the residual waste should be disposed of in a manner appropriate to local landscape and site conditions, by means of backfilling into abandoned sections, or by progressive site restoration.[143]

Similar ravages result from quarrying for granite and limestone. Modern road-construction methods, the use of mass-produced building materials, and the unending possibilities for utilizing pre-cast concrete sections, have encouraged an extensive demand for crushed granite and limestone. Again, the 12 limestone quarries either in or near the National Park are considerable employers within their surrounding communities. There are also active granite quarries at Shap and Threlkeld. They are prominent in the landscape and may well become dominant as the demand for aggregate grows – this could be given an immediate boost if the Windscale nuclear power-station and its ancillary services undertake large new building operations. In the Peak District National Park the growth of limestone extraction had particularly acute effects. Weathered limestone pavements are also attractive to seekers of rockery stone. A number in the north-west have already been devastated; for instance, parts of Farleton Knott; places in the south of the county in the Arnside and Silverdale area, on Hampsfell above Grange-over-Sands, and on Orton Scar.

If these interesting and attractive areas are to be protected from commercial exploitation, and if their rich flora is to survive, the planning authorities must have stronger powers, as recommended in the 1976 Stevens Report *Planning Control over Mineral Working* and the Verney Report of the Advisory Committee on Aggregates (also 1976). At the moment a landowner can claim he is pursuing a policy of agricultural improvement (not requiring planning permission) if the stone is being removed without mechanical aids. This loophole has allowed the destruction to continue in at least one area of Cumbria. It is now suggested that there should be powers to designate limestone pavement areas, in much the same way as Tree Preservation Orders are made, or buildings of importance are 'listed'.

The old mining and quarrying activities often leave abandoned derelict sites. These can be important to industrial archaeologists, but need careful restoration schemes with appropriate after-uses considered. An example is the Greenside lead-mine whose effluent caused so much trouble in polluting Ullswater. Similar situations at the Threlkeld lead mine, Embleton granite quarry, Tilberthwaite Ghyll quarry, and Uzzicar Mine and screes are being investigated. They may require simple treatment only, or work carried out on a larger scale for a specific after-use. This has to be undertaken with due concern for conservation interests and safe public access.

We have noted the early use of electricity at the Greenside mine before the turn of the present century. No industrial enterprise can avoid the use of electrical power, and the gradual spread of rural electrification has also brought many benefits to farms and isolated communities. Getting the wires there caused many arguments.

The first grid supply of electricity to the Lake District came to Keswick about 1890, but connections to it by the private companies thereafter were slow and fragmented.[144] Before and after the First World War the concern was, understandably, to supply profitable areas, i.e. the towns. But in 1926 the Electricity (Supply) Act charged its Commissioners with certain duties, one of which was to prepare the North-West England and North Wales Electricity Scheme (1928).

A main grid-line of 132,000 volts was to enter Cumberland, pass to the west of Penrith, and extend to Carlisle. The county town was designated for generating, whilst at Penrith the main supply would be stepped down for transmission at 33,000 volts. This secondary transmission line was planned in a direct line, passing Penruddock, and at Braithwaite cutting across the Brackenthwaite Fells, the Vale of Lorton, via Cleator Moor to Whitehaven. The next scheme, in October 1928 was for a ring line which linked Whitehaven and Workington, taking the line on to Carlisle via Aspatria and Wigton.

Originally the Penrith to Cleator Moor section in this second scheme was shown in a straight line and objections were raised over its route through the Whinlatter Pass. A third route was proposed, exchanging the Whinlatter Pass for the Wythop Valley. This route also became the subject of negotiation – frequently met thereafter – about burying the cables in the Keswick area. Alternatives were put forward to simplify the routes, and provide a coastal loop rather than hazardous mountain ones.[145] But there were still great gaps and inadequacies and each suggested route was bitterly debated. A new enemy was threatening the scenery, and the first big issue arose in the summer of 1937 over the Borrowdale line.

The Mid Cumberland Electricity Company proposed an 11,000 volt line via Catbells to the Honister Quarries on one of two routes: a) over National Trust land, or b) behind Castle Crag to Rosthwaite. A meeting was held in August 1937 to discuss the best route for the line, and the possibility of undergrounding parts of it. The Company offered a pound for every pound raised by public subscription towards the cost of laying part of the line underground. After much discussion of the principle involved and of the risk of the Company withdrawing its offer if forced to a public inquiry, the F.L.D. Committee first agreed to organize a public appeal for money for this purpose.[146] However the National Trust, the C.P.R.E., and Mr Norman Birkett strongly disapproved of making any appeal on the basis of the Company's offer.

Finally F.L.D., after consideration of the principles and of possible tactics rejected the Electricity Company's offer of providing half the total cost, and a meeting was arranged between the Company and the societies involved. In cautious mood the Company refused to modify its figures, or disclose the basis of its costs, and refused to consider an offer limited to the extra cost of low tension distribution to the villages. Whilst £650 had already been promised by private individuals towards the £1,000 offered to the Company, events were moving against the erection of the line.

The contract between the Electricity Company and the Buttermere Green Slate Company, the reason for taking the line into Borrowdale, with the possible spin-off of village supply, lapsed, and it was felt the whole Borrowdale Scheme would be dropped. The F.L.D. was warned that it would be accused of having obstructed the supply of electricity to the villages, and so prepared a statement of its negotiations, with costings attached. In the meantime the Westmorland Electricity Company agreed to bury the high tension line in the neighbourhood of Side Farm in Patterdale.

During the winter of 1937 every householder in Borrowdale signed a petition to the Electricity Commissioners asking for an underground supply. The Company had meanwhile told Cockermouth Rural District Council that there could be no undergrounding of electricity supplies even in areas of special beauty. The Post Office, perhaps mindful of opposition, arranged quietly to bury its telephone lines north of Rosthwaite and near Grange-in-Borrowdale. A new agent of the Electricity Company, just as quietly, was offering householders in Borrowdale a new scheme (unspecified), and taking their answers to questions about whether they would use current, whether they objected to an overhead supply, and whether they would grant wayleaves.

By contrast the gap in the 11,000 volt line between Threlkeld and Penruddock was to be filled by a carefully sited line which met with full approval from everyone, despite the same company being involved. Certain wayleaves proved difficult to obtain, but the outbreak of the Second World War pushed it all into the background, and the Borrowdale matter did not arise again until the spring of 1945.

The Slate Company again applied to the Mid Cumberland Electricity Supply Company for current at as early a date as was possible. The legal position seemed somewhat different to that of 1937 and F.L.D. was watching the situation with extra caution, as just after the war the Dower and Hobhouse Committees were at work on recommendations for setting up National Parks. However by late 1946 it seemed that there was no likelihood of an electricity supply in Borrowdale during the next two or three years. Then came the legislation to nationalize the electricity supply industry, through the implementation of the Electricity Act 1947.

In Lakeland it meant absorbing eight local authority undertakings, eight company undertakings, and four non-statutory ones controlling supply from the Scottish border to North Lancashire, and from the West Riding of Yorkshire to West Cumberland.[147] Vesting day, 1 April 1948, saw the emergence of the North West Electricity Board. It was soon realized, for the first time, that on nationalization only 2,217 farms and other premises in their area were connected to the main supply. It was necessary to lay down two successive five-year programmes to make inroads into the backlog of rural electrification.

The Board was soon to be involved in fierce arguments over whether transmission lines should be carried overhead or put underground in many areas of scenic beauty, including Martindale, Langdale, Borrowdale, and Eskdale. But firstly a word about the problems associated with undergrounding transmission lines. The main considerations are cost, efficient insulation, and the need for terminal works at points of changeover from overhead to underground sections. These could in some cases be more objectionable than the continuous overhead line.[148] Even in 1959 the cost per mile of a 275 kilovolt double circuit overhead line was £25,000, compared with a cost of around £400,000 per mile for underground cables of similar carrying capacity. However it was pointed out at the time this statement was made that in the countryside it was the undergrounding of a much lower voltage line that was of more immediate concern.[149]

Such arguments were given a sharp twist in the Lake District in 1947 by a scheme to extend the existing high-tension line from Beckfoot Quarry in Eskdale some 300 yd to the Guest House of the Co-operative Holidays Association. The wild beauty of Eskdale had attracted previous attention in 1938, when a public appeal to raise £1,480 was launched to compensate the Forestry Commission for not afforesting 740 acres of plantable land. It was obvious that overhead distribution in the central part of Eskdale would be a serious injury, but it was agreed as a temporary measure in the hope that an overhead line on from the guest house to the village of Boot could be avoided. The County Planning Authority supported F.L.D. in this objection; but both were soon involved in a more serious controversy – a proposed hydro-electric scheme for Upper Eskdale and the Duddon.

Prior to local government reorganization in 1974 many services in the Barrow peninsula were the responsibility of Lancashire County Council. A firm of consultant engineers had reported in 1947 that the most satisfactory and comprehensive water scheme would be to build an 80ft dam and reservoir above Seathwaite in the Duddon valley. This proposal in turn became merged into a larger one, put forward by the Corporation of Barrow-in-Furness, for a hydro-electric scheme to displace the coal-burning generating station at Barrow. Reservoirs were suggested under Cam Spout Crag above the main Esk falls, and above the other falls of the Esk in Lingcove Beck, each reservoir being made accessible by a full-scale road from the foot of Hard Knott to the sites of the two dams. These would be at about the 1,400 ft contour line, for the water to be piped in an aqueduct over Hard Knott Pass (summit 1,290 ft), and so down the Duddon to the high ground above the gorge. The rocky sub-soil would necessitate pipes overground, not buried, with the consequent need to remove much in their path.

The first power-station was to be set on this high ground near the Duddon gorge, with the water discharged through it filling a reservoir in the hanging valley over High Pitchers, above Seathwaite village. The falls from Seathwaite Tarn would feed a second power-station, and through it would discharge into the same reservoir. From this reservoir the outflow would be piped through a third power-station, into a fourth reservoir near Seathwaite, a fourth power-station being put lower down the Duddon near Ulpha. The four power-stations would be in series linked by pylons (not transmission lines on wooden poles), and from the Ulpha power-station the march of the pylons would be continued down-valley to the sea. It was an ambitious scheme calculated to arouse the rhetoric of the sleeping Wordsworth and Ruskin, and of all lovers of the Lake District. Fortunately it did not come about. Barrow instead replaced its intake in the River Duddon above Ulpha, with Seathwaite Tarn as the town's main source of supply. This rendered the use of the same water for a hydro-electric scheme unnecessary, and there was wonder at it ever being suggested.

Mention has been made of the North West Electricity Board's involvement, taken over from private undertakings, to supply power to Martindale, Langdale, Borrowdale, and Eskdale. In May 1951 the Board stated that its policy would be to 'concentrate its limited capital on those projects which benefit the largest number of people':[150] none of the valley projects could be held to satisfy that requirement, or so it seemed. Abandoning yet again the Borrowdale and Langdale lines they proposed supplying, by overhead line, three farms in Martindale. The Westmorland planning authority was unwilling to concede anything other than an underground line, and the case came to a 'hearing' (as provided by Section 21 of the Electricity Act 1919) in July 1951 before an Inspector of the Ministry of Fuel and Power.

At this hearing the Board restated that it would not construct an underground line, quoting costs of £1,455 for overhead, and £6,787 for underground supply. After a delay of almost a year the Minister of Fuel and Power gave his decision in favour of the Electricity Board's proposal to serve the Martindale farms by means of an overhead line. This decision was against the planning authority, and equally against the voluntary societies who had supported careful treatment in a valley of great beauty. The Minister urged, lamely, that the route chosen for the overhead line should be as inconspicuous as possible, but it was only after considerable argument that a route along the lower slopes of the fell-side was chosen, where the poles, not being seen against the skyline, are much less conspicuous. This sort of solution was later adopted in other dales (such as Longsleddale), with satisfactory results.

On 19 June 1953 the Minister of Fuel and Power announced the Government's decision to approve a further increase of £1½ million in the capital available for rural electrification in England and Wales in the following 18 months.[151] It increased the money available in 1954 to £7½ million and it did much to alter, slowly, the intransigent attitudes of the Area Electricity Boards. The average return to the Board from an individual consumer in the Lakeland areas seemed to be about one-twelfth of the cost of connection to the supply. There were two important considerations; the first was that unless the benefits of electricity could be brought to rural communities, then the process of rural depopulation would be inevitably hastened. Secondly, where, by appropriate national action a tract of country widely famed for its natural beauty was set aside as a National Park for the benefit of the nation at large, then providing a supply of electricity without disfigurement and damage should be solved by a national policy, and any extra expense should be defrayed nationally.

The long-drawn-out campaign over the Borrowdale supply, which had started in 1937, was given a jolt forward in June 1955. The North West Electricity Board finally announced that it had decided to underground the whole of the much-debated line up Borrowdale, for the distance between Keswick and Rosthwaite, including a loop line along the far side of Derwent Water. Behind the scenes the National Parks Commission had made representations to the Minister, not only about the Lake District electrification but also about other areas of the country where similar difficulties were being experienced.[152] That the line was not to be wholly underground was due to a Planning Board decision 'that in their view it was not essential that the whole of the Borrowdale line should be underground'.[153] It finally transpired that in spite of representations to the Ministry of Fuel and Power, and a visit by a Ministry officer, no decision was made. The Electricity Board therefore decided to lay the whole of the line underground, a surprising turn-about which silenced the most vocal.

The Planning Board said it had differed from the National Parks Commission in this Borrowdale decision because it had a duty to safeguard the supply of essential services for the people of the Lake District, as well as its traditional landscape beauty. The need for a national policy was clearly desirable, especially in view of the Borrowdale issues. Despite all the assurances the old threat of a financial crisis was enough reason for a delay to the work. The matter was raised with the Electricity Board in Manchester, and a policy statement issued which seemed to have great perils for the Borrowdale supply. In essence the Electricity Board stated that it could not consider the Borrowdale or any other scheme in isolation from the rest of rural development in the northwestern area. Each scheme would also have to be judged according to its capital cost in relation to the overall amount allocated for rural development, the revenue return on each scheme, and the number of consumers to be covered and the nature of their requirements. Furthermore, 'zoning' was to be introduced to ensure equal treatment of areas.[154]

It seemed to be a policy likely to delay indefinitely the provision of an electricity supply to a scattered rural population where the income could be expected to be very small in contrast to the capital expenditure. Fierce lobbying, with a recognition that the Electricity Board was working under national financial restraints, resulted in a start being promised on the first instalment of the Borrowdale scheme, that is, a supply to Grange-in-Borrowdale in the financial year 1956–7.

Proposals for a supply to Deepdale, near Patterdale, although less complicated than the Borrowdale issue, were hardly more reassuring. Local agreement had been reached that part of the line could be constructed overhead, but the National Parks Commission subsequently made representations to the Ministry that the whole of the Deepdale line should be laid underground. It was a difficult conflict of duty – the national body acting as it thought best, the local Planning Board having to comply with duties laid on it not only by the National Parks Act, but to secure the development of public utility services in its area under the Town and Country Planning Acts. The issues were the safeguarding of natural beauty, and the need for the supply of electricity to the dale farms, cottages, and other properties. To insist on underground lines only would be to deprive many Lake District people, residents and visitors alike, of an electricity supply for many years to come.

In the case of Upper Langdale the conflict went to appeal, and the Minister gave his approval of the Planning Board's recommendation: that in addition to the underground lengths offered by the Electricity Board a further 600 yd should be laid underground. It had however taken four months for the decision to be reached after the appeal hearing. By contrast to these electricity supply issues, the Post Office was being helpful over a number of cases touching both new and old telephone lines, in Wasdale, and beside Ullswater, between Glencoyne and Aira Green. The Planning Board recorded its appreciation of the care the Post Office was exercising, not only in siting lines, but in agreeing that the new Wasdale exchange should be built with a covering of cement rendering to match the local stone and a slate roof. They had also shown consideration by avoiding the use of the bright red telephone box in attractive landscape.

In negotiations over rural electrification years seemed to pass with routine improvements and few decisions of moment. A supply reached Buttermere in 1959 having been carried almost entirely underground near the foot of Crummock Water, but in 1961 the matter of putting the Upper Borrowdale line underground, as the Electricity Board had done in Lower Borrowdale, was again raised. Once more agreement could not be reached on the treatment of the spur line to Stonethwaite, and accordingly, after reference to the Ministry of Power, a Public Inquiry was held at Rosthwaite in February 1961.

Three months later the Minister issued his decision on the various lengths of line over and under ground, and upheld the recommendation that the supply from Chapel House to Stonethwaite should be put underground. A month later, enigmatically, the Electricity Board announced its decision to lay the whole line underground. The situation had improved enormously, and with the whole of the Borrowdale valley served by a completely underground system possibilities for co-operation seemed better than for many years past.

By 1966 virtual completion of rural electrification of the Lake District was a fact, and the Electricity Board asked for recommendations from the Planning Board on the undergrounding of overhead distribution lines when there was an obvious gain to local amenity. In the case of one main supply line in the Martindale valley, the subject of earlier dispute, undergrounding was requested by the planning authority. It was however not carried out. For five years, 1965–70, electricity as a subject dropped out of the Planning Board's annual reports. Various schemes of improvement were carried out quietly – at Lakeside, Hesket Newmarket, and Bassenthwaite for example – with a resulting benefit in the National Park, and in the attitude of the relevant authorities involved.

For more than a decade in fact the Electricity Board had not been confronted with a public inquiry into the route of an overhead electricity line. The early struggles of the late fifties and early sixties, when the supply of electricity to the countryside was proceeding apace – the most contentious being the Borrowdale valley supply – seemed well past. However towards the end of 1975 the Electricity Board proposed to construct a 33 kilovolt overhead line between Windermere and Ambleside.

Objection was made by the National Trust, F.L.D. and a number of land-owners to a length of the line above the Lowwood Hotel, close to the north-eastern shore of the lake. Unfortunately the Special Planning Board had agreed to the route prior to the inquiry held in December 1975. The area involved was one of special beauty with views across Windermere to the Langdale Pikes and the central mountains of the Lake District. Six months or so later the Secretary of State for the Department of Energy refused consent to the North West Electricity Board to put the line overhead between Holbeck and Dove Nest – the attractively barge-boarded house high above the Lake, where Mrs Hemans wrote the immortal *The Boy Stood on the Burning Deck*. It was estimated to cost an additional £52,667 to put the line underground for this section.[155] In earlier years this would have been a crucial point in refusing the improvement.

In spring 1977 work started on taking an electricity supply to the head of Wasdale, one of the most wild and dramatic places in the Lake District, and one of the few hamlets without such a supply. After careful examination it was decided to put two and a half miles of the cable on the bed of the lake, to underground a similar length, and to overhead two short lengths where the screening was adequate. It was a good solution in an area of wild beauty.

Government policy on unusual costs of this kind had been set out in 1976.[156] It stated that where a National Park Authority required a service line to be underground, the additional cost should be borne by the Electricity Board and the Park Authority in proportions to be negotiated for each case. The Country-side Commission in the Wasdale matter made a contribution of £27,000 in grant-aid, and the remaining sum towards the £75,000 total cost was provided by the National Trust, the Electricity Board, and the inhabitants of the valley.

But Wasdale was not the last place in the Lake District to receive a mains supply. Watendlath was connected a few months afterwards. As both these isolated communities waited, more ominous issues were focusing in the after-math of the mammoth public inquiry held at Whitehaven in 1977. This was to examine the planning applications by British Nuclear Fuels Ltd to expand the nuclear site and power station at Windscale not far from the cliffs of St Bees, and the Victorian resort of Seascale. It is visible from Haycock, Seatallan, the shoulders of those hills that face westwards, from the summit and the slopes of Harter Fell in Eskdale, and from the mountains to the north of Hardknott Pass. Black against the shining sea, and with approval for the expansion sub-sequently granted, there must be many wondering whether the west wind will carry, finally, more than the sweet scent of heather and bracken. The Lake District is still at risk from man's uncertainty about his complex future, and the way he grapples with its intricate patterns.

VII Conclusion

In the earliest editions of *Walking in the Lake District* H. H. Symonds urged the need for 'some thoroughly national group of Friends of the Lake District to supply the emotional impetus without which skill and knowledge win no victories'. A Society was established in 1934 under the name he suggested and was active and articulate in the days when planning law was weak and ideas about when and how to protect the environment were unformed. Many damaging proposals would have been implemented, without comment, if F.L.D. and other amenity bodies had not existed to voice concern and objection. It has been shown that as a consequence of their activities much has been prevented that would today have marred the Lake District landscape, and much has been modified that would otherwise have gone ahead on a devastating scale. For the Lake District has nurtured a strong protective spirit, perhaps greater than in any other part of England, and in consequence its beauty remains but little violated. Nevertheless, it cannot be said that all is well. There is no reason to believe that the threats and pressures of the future will be any less than those of the past century; all the indications are to the contrary.

It was here in the Lake District that many principles of conservation were first voiced and developed: indeed, the history of conservation in the Lake District is to a large extent the history of conservation in Britain. As a result of Lake District experience it became generally accepted that uncontrolled exploitation of the countryside for economic ends could not be tolerated. Quite the reverse; resources, both money and effort, must be devoted to conservation. For example we cannot afford to abstract water in the cheapest possible manner; if water abstraction is unavoidable then money must be spent on minimizing its impact by, for example, building pumping stations underground, as was done at Pooley Bridge on Ullswater and at Calgarth on Windermere. The same principle has influenced the means of providing electricity. In the Lake District it has become standard practice to lay lines underground or along carefully selected overland routes, instead of conventional, cheaper, but scenically damaging alternatives.

As early as the 1930s F.L.D. was arguing that traffic policy in the Lake District should not be based on the philosophy of providing for the rapid movement of vehicles. F.L.D. maintained that the management of traffic, not the construction of new, wider, straighter, and faster highways, was the least damaging solution to traffic problems. This opinion has met with only partial acceptance; major roads have been constructed, the A66 for example, but it has been agreed that the minor and dale-head roads should remain substantially as they are.

The Lake District has been fortunate in being administered by an Authority more effective and independent than those of most Parks. Apart from the Lake District, only the Peak District National Park is controlled by a Board rather than a County Council Committee. When the Lake District National Park was established in 1951 the Board was composed of four representatives from each of the three County Councils whose areas then divided the Park – Cumberland, Westmorland, and Lancashire – together with six persons appointed by the Secretary of State. This constitution gave the board an independence that was lost when in 1974, as a result of local government reorganization, the whole of the Park fell within one County – Cumbria. The new Planning Board of 27 members, 18 appointed by the County Council and 9 by the Secretary of State for the Environment, is potentially subservient to the interests of the County Council. Indeed, National Park purposes and the Board's duties have at times been subject to the whim of a dominant political party.

It is of the greatest importance not to forget that the Lake District is a *National* Park, designated for the benefit of the Nation, and financed largely from the national Exchequer; only a small amount (less than 10 per cent) is borne by the Cumbrian ratepayer. There are therefore strong grounds for arguing that the Lake District Special Planning Board should be strengthened and made securely independent by legislation to produce a Board composed equally of County Council nominees and Ministerial nominees, the latter chosen for experience relevant to the needs of the National Park.

The Lake District is a unique English landscape that has influenced our culture in art and literature, and given spiritual inspiration and renewal to innumerable people. It is an asset of inestimable value demanding the highest degree of protection, and protect it we must, with all our strength, if we are to keep this nook of England free from rash assault.

Notes to Part One

1 J. D. Marshall *Furness and the Industrial Revolution* (1958); Oliver Wood 'The Development of the Coal, Iron and Shipbuilding Industries of West Cumberland', unpublished Ph.D thesis, London University 1952

2 John K. Walton 'The Windermere Tourist Trade in the Age of the Railway, 1847–1912' in *Windermere in the Nineteenth Century* Lancaster University N.W. Regional Studies Centre, Occasional Paper I (1976) p. 23

3 Mary Moorman *William Wordsworth: A Biography* (1965) vol. 2 pp. 561–4

4 Harriet Martineau *A Complete Guide to the English Lakes* (1855) p. 3

5 Victoria Ch 46–7, 1883

6 An indefatigable fighter in this and other amenity societies was the Kendal shoe manufacturer Robert Somervell (1851–1933). For further information about him see his *Chapters of Autobiography*, edited by his sons (1935)

7 *Westmorland Gazette*, letters in issues dated 3 January, 7 February, 7, 14, 21 March 1885

8 Material on both societies at the Cumbria County Record Office, Kendal, ref. WDX 269

9 *Westmorland Gazette* 5 September 1885

10 Eleanor F. Rawnsley *Canon Rawnsley: An Account of his Life* (1923) p. 70

11 See Alan Hankinson *Camera on the Crags: a Portfolio of Early Rock Climbing Photographs by the Abraham Brothers* (1975)

12 John Dower *National Parks in England and Wales* Ministry of Town and Country Planning Cmd 6628 (1945)

13 See Lake District Special Planning Board *National Park Plan* Section I (1978)

14 The main electrified line from London to Glasgow passes to the east of the Lake District, and the line to the Barrow peninsula across the Kent Estuary to the south.

15 See Carlisle Public library, leaflets on the Thirlmere Defence Association and James Mansergh *The Thirlmere Water Scheme of the Manchester Corporation*

16 See Robert Somervell *Autobiography* (1935)

17 See Sir John Harwood *History and Description of the Thirlmere Water Scheme* (1895)

18 *The Times* 20 October 1877

19 Ibid.

20 Eleanor F. Rawnsley *Canon Rawnsley* (1923) ch. V 'Manchester Water Supply'

21 *Westmorland Gazette* 27 March 1886 p. 2

22 Ibid. p. 3

23 A factual and unemotional account was given by the Engineer-in-charge, Sir John Harwood, in his *History and Description of the Thirlmere Water Scheme* (1895)

24 *Westmorland Gazette* 4 July 1885, p. 5

25 Eleanor F. Rawnsley *Canon Rawnsley* (1923); also notes gathered by Susan Symonds, 'The Defence of the Lake District 1875–1913' in the F.L.D. archives

26 In all, Manchester obtained eight Private Acts of Parliament from 1879 to 1954 in order that it could pursue its abstractions of water from the Lake District.

27 Noted in Sir John Harwood *History and Description of the Thirlmere Water Scheme* (1895) p. 124

28 The English Lake District Association stated that one of its objects was 'to maintain in good order existing roads and footpaths' *Westmorland Gazette* 24 January 1885

29 See D. & J. Hay *Mardale – The Drowned Village* (1976)

30 Lady (D. S.) Simon *A Century of City Government* (1947) p. 356

31 F. L. D. *News-Letter* August 1972 p. 7

32 E.g. North West Water Authority *Water Resources in Cumbria* (1976)

33 Susan J. Dolby, 'The Politics of Manchester's Water Supply 1961–7', unpublished M.A. thesis, Manchester University 1968

34 F.L.D. *News-Letter* July 1963 p. 4

35 The most significant of the physical checks was the refusal to leave to construct a second tunnel with the consequent saving of Longsleddale valley from engineering works. In addition the Lake should not be drawn down below its natural level.

36 F.L.D. *News-Letter* July 1979 p. 9. Given that degree of abstraction the water level would probably have fallen and risen between 9 and 11 ft, according to weather conditions.

37 See Thomas Gray *Journal in the Lakes* (1769)

38 The Marshall family of Monk Coniston established plantations from 1820 onwards in Patterdale, Buttermere, near Derwent Water, and at Monks Coniston. They used the strain of larch introduced by the Duke of Atholl on his Scottish estates. See W. H. Pearsall and W. H. Pennington *The Lake District* (The New Naturalist series) (1973) p. 264

39 See John Housman *A Descriptive Tour and Guide to the Lakes* 2nd edn (1802)

40 See Norman Nicholson *The Lakes, the Adventures of the First Tourists* (1955) and Edmund W. Hodge *Enjoying the Lakes: from Post-chaise to National Park* (1957)

41 R. V. Lennard 'Woods in the Lakeland Landscape' *The Estate Magazine* 20 September 1943

42 William Wordsworth *Guide to the Lakes* (1835) p. 86. The authors have used the Oxford (1970) edition edited by E. de Sélincourt.

43 G. E. Mingay *English Landed Society in the Eighteenth Century* (1963) p. 57

44 J. D. Marshall and M. Davies-Shiel *The Industrial Archaeology of the Lake Counties* 2nd edn (1977) pp. 60–88

45 See Forestry Commission *14th Annual Report* (1933)

46 Forestry Commission *Thornthwaite* (1951) p. 9

47 F.L.D. Minutes, October 1934

48 R. V. Lennard 'Forestry and the Lake District' *The Nineteenth Century and After* vol. cxvii, April 1935 p. 473

49 *The Times* 19 February 1935. See also articles by Arthur Gardner in *The Spectator* 1 March 1935 and Kenneth Spence in the *Manchester Guardian* 7 February 1935.

50 *National Parks in England and Wales* Cmd 6628 (1945)

51 *Afforestation in the Lake District* report by the Joint Informal Committee of the Forestry Commission and C.P.R.E. (1936)

52 F.L.D. Minutes, July 1936

53 H. H. Symonds *Afforestation in the Lake District* (1936); Forestry Commission *Agreements on Afforestation in the Lake District* (1955); Michael A. McCarthy 'The Politics of Pressure – an Analysis of the Methodology of an Environmental Pressure Group' [F.L.D.] unpublished M.A. thesis, Keele University 1976 pp. 28–31

54 They were Lawrence Chubb, Patrick Abercrombie, E. N. Buxton, G. A. Jellicoe, W. Harding Thompson, H. J. Tozer, and G. M. Trevelyan.

55 The Company was established in 1937 to acquire farms with the purpose of maintaining traditional farming and preserving traditional farm-buildings. See F.L.D. *News-Letter* Autumn 1977 p. 14

56 Appeal leaflet, F.L.D. Minutes, November 1940

57 Forestry Commission *Report of the National Forest Park Committee* [Hardknott] (1945) p. 7

58 Ibid. p. 3

59 Reported in F.L.D. Minutes, November 1942

60 Ibid., September 1943

61 F.L.D. *News-Letter* August 1954 pp. 2–3

62 Forestry Commission *Agreements on Afforestation in the Lake District* (1955)

63 F.L.D. *News-Letter* August 1955 pp. 10–11

64 *Report of the National Parks Committee (England and Wales)* (1947) p. 86

65 Lake District Special Planning Board *The Broadleaved Woodlands of the Lake District* (1978) p. 21

66 *Report of the National Park Policies Review Committee* (1974) p. 86

67 Ibid., p. 65, where it was recommended that the afforestation of bare land in a National Park should be brought within planning control. Some members of the Committee also felt that forestry operations, felling and replanting, should also come under control. The Government did not accept this view (Circular 4/76); F.L.D. *News-Letter* September 1974, p. 3

68 H. H. Symonds *Afforestation in the Lake District* (1936) pp. 39–50

69 See R. Miles *Forestry in the English Landscape* (1967)

70 *Westmorland Gazette* 22 December 1978 p. 5

71 These comments are based on the invaluable and carefully researched book by L. A. Williams *Road Transport in Cumbria in the Nineteenth Century* (1975) pp. 12, 27

72 John K. Walton, 'The Windermere Tourist Trade in the Age of the Railway, 1847–1912' in *Windermere in the Nineteenth Century* Lancaster University N.W. Regional Studies Centre, Occasional Paper I (1976) pp. 19–38; Geoffrey Beard *The Greater House in Cumbria* (1978) pp. 36–7

73 L. A. Williams *Road Transport in Cumbria in the Nineteenth Century* p. 199, fn. 74

74 Alan Hankinson *Camera on the Crags – A Portfolio of Early Rock Climbing by the Abraham Brothers* (1975) p. 20

75 Irvine Hunt (ed.) *Fenty's Album* (1975) pp. 18–20

76 F.L.D. *A Road Policy for the Lake District* (1939) p. i

77 Ibid. p. 6

78 H. H. Symonds *Walking in the Lake District* 1st edn (1933) p. 48

79 Based on F.L.D. Minutes, 1936–7 and P. A. Abercrombie and S. A. Kelly *Cumbrian Regional Planning Scheme* (1932).

It was noted in the latter (p. 200) that when 'fog horns, devised to be heard for miles at sea have actually been installed in motor cars the absolute necessity for action is apparent'. Adequate silencers for motor cycles were also urged.

80 P. A. Abercrombie and S. A. Kelly *Cumbrian Regional Planning Scheme* p. 47

81 The construction grants were normally 60 per cent of improvement to a Class 1 road, and 50 per cent for a Class 2 road. A full explanation of all the relevant restrictive clauses in the Road Traffic Act 1930, and the Restriction of Ribbon Development Act is given in the F.L.D. booklet *A Road Policy for the Lake District* (1939)

82 Cited in F.L.D. *A Road Policy for the Lake District* (1961)

83 Colin Buchanan *Traffic in Towns: A Study of the Long Term Problems of Traffic in Urban Areas* (1963) p. 17

84 Lake District Planning Report *8th Annual Report 1959–60* p. 5

85 The National Park Policies Review Committee, headed by Lord Sandford, recommended in its *Report* (1974) p. 84 'that Park authorities as well as the other planning authorities should contribute to the planning of the road system for the region in which the park is situated'.

86 The *Manchester Guardian* 19 February 1965

87 F.L.D. *News-Letter* September 1965 pp. 10–11

88 John Dower *National Parks in England and Wales* Cmd 6628 (1945)

89 Gerald Haythornthwaite *The Case against the A66 Proposals* C.P.R.E. (1972); D.O.E. *Report of the A66 (Penrith) Public Inquiry* (1972); Michael A. McCarthy 'The Politics of Influence – An Analysis of the Methodology of an Environmental Pressure Group' [F.L.D.] unpublished M.A. thesis, Keele University 1976 pp. 206–305.

90 See Alan F. Holford-Walker *Proof of Evidence – Proposed Improvements between Fitz Cottage and East of Highgate* C.P.R.E. (1972).

91 F.L.D. archives. Divisional Road Engineer (M.O.T.) to Geoffrey Berry 30 April 1968

92 F.L.D. *The Lake District Threatened with a Major Industrial Highway* (1972)

93 *Westmorland Gazette* 2 February 1970

94 John Cornforth 'The Threat to Levens Park' *Country Life* 9 January 1969 pp. 62–3; F.L.D. *News-Letter* June 1970 pp. 9–10

95 Hugh Wilson and J. Lewis Womersley *The Barrow Link Road – the Impact on the Arnside/Silverdale Area of Outstanding Natural Beauty* (1970).

96 The Morecambe Bay Barrage Water Scheme, which did not proceed, but had been planned to incorporate a road.

97 H. Wilson and J. L. Womersley *Traffic Management in the Lake District National Park* (1972)

98 The Countryside Commission's reluctance to commit itself to a definite attitude prior to the A66 inquiry, is noted in M. A. McCarthy 'The Politics of Influence' unpublished M.A. thesis, Keele University 1976 p. 241 and R. Kimber and J. J. Richardson *Pressure Groups in Britain – a Reader* (1974) pp. 183–5

99 *Summit* October 1971

100 *The Economist* 25 October 1969

101 *The Financial Times* 18 September 1970

102 Harold Wilson *The Labour Government 1964–70–A Personal Record* (1971) p. 766

103 H. Simpson and J. A. Zetter *West Cumberland Trunk Road Study* Countryside Commission and Lake District Planning Board (1972) paras. 124–5

104 E. W. Hodge 'Is the Lake District Over-Protected?' *Town and Country Planning* December 1971

105 Quoted in F.L.D. *News-Letter* February 1973 p. 2

106 Gerald Haythornthwaite *Approval of the Draft Orders for the Expansion of the A66: a Note* (1973)

107 The *Guardian* 28 December 1972

108 F.L.D. *News-Letter* Autumn 1978; p. 15 notes the prohibition on certain sections of the A591

109 F.L.D. *News-Letter* October 1975 pp. 6–7

110 F.L.D. *News-Letter* February 1974 p. 12

111 Norman Nicholson *The Lakes, the Adventures of the First Tourists* (1955); Edmund W. Hodge *Enjoying the Lakes: From Post-chaise to National Park* (1957)

112 Edmund W. Hodge *Enjoying the Lakes* (1957) pp. 191–2

113 *The Right to Roam: the Rambler and the Countryside* The Ramblers' Association (1964) p. 13

114 G. Tansey 'The Lake District and its relationship to the North as a whole' in *Whither the Lake District?* discussions sponsored and published by Ambleside Rotary Club (1968) pp. 110–11

115 Lake District Planning Board *1st Annual Report* 1951–3 (1953) p. 25

116 Countryside Commission *Digest of Countryside Recreation Statistics* (1969) p. 11

117 Gordon E. Cherry *Environmental Planning 1939–1969* vol. II *National Parks and Recreation in the Countryside* (1975) p. 51

118 W. B. Yapp *The Weekend Motorist in the Lake District* Countryside Commission (1969) p. 17; H. Wilson and L. Womersley *Traffic Management in the Lake District National Park* F.L.D. (1972) p. 82

119 Cumberland Countryside Conference *Caravan and Camping Sites: Working Party Report* (1972)

120 Lake District Special Planning Board *23rd Annual Report* 1974–5 pp. 10–12

121 Barbara Hall *The Royal Windermere Yacht Club 1860–1960* (1960) p. 18

122 Lake District Special Planning Board *23rd Annual Report* 1974–5 pp. 9–10

123 Local authorities have power under Section 76 of the Public Health Act 1961 to make by-laws dealing with noise from power boats, and requiring engines to be fitted with efficient silencers.

124 F.L.D. *News-Letter* Autumn 1978 pp. 22–4. A North West Water Authority by-law of 1 January 1977 also required boats using Windermere to avoid discharging sanitary waste into the lake.

125 The Rambler's Association *People and the Countryside* (1971) p. 8

126 Manchester Corporation *Recreation at Haweswater: Working Party Report* (n.d. – 1974)

127 Lake District Special Planning Board *23rd Annual Report* 1974–5 p. 16

128 Forestry Commission map 'Walking in Ennerdale Forest' (n.d. – 1975?)

129 Bruce and Margaret Hay *Brathay, the first twenty-five Years, 1947–1972* (1972)

130 The paths, gates, and stone walls on the slopes of Helvellyn are an example, and are referred to in a consultative report *The Management of Glenridding Common and Greenside Mine* issued by the Lake District Special Planning Board (1978) p. 13. At Tarn Hows the National Trust had to take further steps to divert walkers in order to preserve the green slopes. Further development of the Grizedale Forest is being discouraged to avoid spoiling the character of the area. See the leader 'The Not-So-Lonely Hills' in *Westmorland Gazette* 8 December 1978

131 Countryside Commission *The Lake District Upland Management Experiment* (1976)

132 J. D. Marshall and Michael Davies-Shiel *Industrial Archaeology of the Lake Counties* 2nd edn (1977) pp. 135–160

133 Galena, mined at Greenside until 1962, is an ore yielding 80 per cent lead and 12 oz silver per ton. From 1839 onwards the company sold its silver output to the Bank of England. See J. D. Marshall and M. Davies-Shiel *Industrial Archaeology of the Lake District* p. 150 Wolframite, the ore from which tungsten is obtained, is found in the Carrock Fell area of the valley. The mine was reopened in 1976 (the detailed planning approvals date from 1972) and the scale of future working needs careful monitoring. See Lake District Special Planning Board *National Park Plan* (1978) p. 173

134 E. Lynn Linton *The Lake Country* (1864) p. 32

135 P. A. Abercrombie and S. A. Kelly *Cumbrian Regional Planning Scheme* (1932) p. 116

136 F. L. D. Minutes, October 1932, pp. 11–12

137 P. A. Abercrombie and S. A. Kelly *Cumbrian Regional Planning Scheme* (1932) p. 121

138 *The Times* 19 January 1940

139 F. L. D. Minutes, 29 July 1941, p. 3

140 J. D. Marshall and M. Davies–Shiel *Industrial Archaeology of the Lake District* (1977) p. 150

141 E. Lynn Linton *The Lake Country* p. 33

142 An application to erect a 10,000 sq. ft slate processing building in the Coniston Copper Mines Valley was refused by the Planning Board in 1974. An appeal was lodged, a public inquiry held in October 1974, and the decision upheld by the Minister. F.L.D. *News-Letter* February 1975 p. 19; October 1975 p. 27

143 Lake District Special Planning Board *National Park Plan* (1978) p. 169

144 A. H. Griffin *New Light in the Lakeland Dales* North West Electricity Board (n.d. – 1965) p. 1

145 P. A. Abercrombie and S. A. Kelly *Cumbrian Regional Planning Scheme* (1932) pp. 31–3

146 F. L. D. Minutes, 1 October 1937 p. 1

147 A. H. Griffin *New Light in the Lakeland Dales* (1965) p. 1

148 Sir Christopher Hinton *Power, Production, and Transmission in the Countryside* Central Electricity Generating Board (1960) pp. 10–11

149 By Mrs John Dower; Sir Christopher Hinton *Power, Production, and Transmission in the Countryside* p. 34

150 *The Times* 30 May 1951

151 Hansard, House of Commons Debates 19 June 1953

152 National Parks Commission *5th Annual Report* (1954); Hansard, House of Commons Debates 27 June 1954

153 Lake District Planning Board *3rd Annual Report* 1954–5 p. 13

154 Lake District Planning Board *4th Annual Report* 1955–6 p. 11

155 F. L. D. *News-Letter* Autumn 1976 p. 23

156 D.o.E. Circular 4/76

PART TWO

1

Thirlmere's dam from the summit of Raven Crag. The dam is a modest construction, built at the end of the last century, which raised the level of the existing lakes by 50 ft. It closed the narrow gap between the rock of Great How and the steep cliff of Raven Crag. Tree-planting on the lower side has hidden the supporting banks of the dam and little is seen of it today from any angle. A motor road crosses the dam from the A591 to the Armboth road and gives fine views up the lake to Dunmail Raise. An impressive and ornate plaque built into the upper structure of the dam declared the work to be that of the Aldermen and Councillors of Manchester Corporation, which commenced on 22 August 1890. Manchester was proud of its supply of pure water from the Lake District, and that from Thirlmere is still of high quality as no development around the lake has taken place. The only buildings that now remain in the catchment area, apart from a few ancient barns, are the farm at Steel End at the head of the valley, secluded Dalehead Hall at Thirlspot, and the little church at Wythburn. The school, public house, and other buildings at Wythburn were demolished about 10 years ago; farms at Armboth and other houses went when the valley was flooded. In this picture the water level is down some 15 ft below sill level, a drop which in other parts of the lake produces a considerable band of sterile stones and mud. Thirlmere during most summers displays scenically damaging, drawn-down conditions.

Thirlmere from above Armboth on the footpath to Watendlath. Across the lake the western slopes of Helvellyn. All the land to be seen in this picture was acquired by Manchester Corporation before the flooding of the valley and is now the property of the North West Water Authority. It runs to the summit of Helvellyn beyond the dark rocky knoll of Browncove Crags on the left. The A591 runs through the trees a little above the shore line. The hard upper line of the planting and the rectangular projection above Wythburn on the right has been much criticized, but in recent years considerable concessions have been made to amenity by selective felling and new planting. The trees on the western side of the lake are more varied and attractive, with stretches of native oak as well as huge and impressive specimens of Douglas fir. About 60 years ago Manchester fenced off large areas to exclude sheep and deer, the primary concern being to conserve the soil on these steep sides by encouraging regeneration. New planting of larch and beech was also carried out. When the afforestation schemes were in their infancy, there was prolonged argument about whether the trees in their maturity would or would not be beneficial to the 'run-off' and 'water-holding' capabilities of the reservoir; in short, whether the evaporation through foliage would be adequately compensated by greater retention of moisture in the soil.

3

Crummock Water from the western shore, looking across to Whiteless Pike and Rannerdale Knotts. The walkers are on the prominent peninsula called Low Ling Crag. The road to Buttermere runs along the far shore. This lake has been used for water supplies since the beginning of the century, at that time for Workington and Cockermouth. In 1953 an Order was sought to increase the abstraction and this was the subject of a public inquiry in December of that year. Up to then the amount taken was small, four million gallons a day, and the works at the outflow near Lanthwaite Woods were modest. The Order provided for an increase of 50 per cent. In addition five million gallons a day had to be allowed to flow down the River Cocker as compensation water. It was contended by the objectors, led by F.L.D., that such levels of abstraction would deplete the lake, with serious damage to its appearance. At the inquiry it was

pointed out that, since the extra water was required primarily for industrial uses, there were ample alternative sources available for Workington without using drinking water of the highest quality and causing damage to the natural beauty of Crummock Water. The Minister of Housing and Local Government accepted this argument and refused to confirm the Order. Another attempt was made in 1963 to take more water from the lake, this time by the West Cumberland Water Board, successor to the former water undertaking. An inquiry was held and subsequently the Minister decided to allow an increase in abstraction to seven million gallons a day. However he disallowed the siting of a new treatment plant beside Scalehill Bridge, which was part of the scheme, and required that a more secluded site should be found. This has been done in the wooded valley a mile below the bridge.

4

Haweswater drawn down to its lowest level since the flooding of the valley. Taken on 30 November 1973 after a light fall of snow. On the left the wooded Riggindale peninsula, beyond which a steep ridge runs up to the highest point of the High Street range. The church and houses of Mardale Green stood to the right of the woods and their ruins can be seen. The valley road continued over the bridge (its parapets are visible) to the Dun Bull Hotel, the site of which is just off the picture to the left. Many people visited Haweswater during the months of 1973 when its past was revealed and there were many nostalgic recollections of life in the valley before the flooding. There are a number of people still living in the Shap, Bampton, and Askham area who recall the old Mardale, which has now assumed a romantic patina. Haweswater, now part of the water-supply complex that includes Ullswater and Wet Sleddale, is particularly susceptible to draw-down. An extensive area of its upper reach beyond the Riggindale peninsula is shallow and frequently exposed, giving it in consequence a desolate appearance. There can be no doubt that a beautiful valley was lost to the Lake District when Mardale was flooded.

5

Haweswater from Harter Fell looking over the Eden valley to the Pennines. The reservoir is drawn down about 30 ft below normal level. There was in the twenties much criticism of Manchester Corporation's acquisition and use of this Lake District valley for water supply. The Thirlmere supply was proving insufficient so Manchester came here for its second reservoir in the Lake District. Mardale was a remote and secluded place, little changed over the centuries. The natural lake of Haweswater was over two miles long, almost divided into two parts at The Straits by a considerable delta at the mouth of the Measand Beck, the two parts being named Low Water (near the entrance to the valley) and High Water (at its mountainous end). There were four working farms in the early thirties, at Chapel Hill, Goosemire, Grove

Brae, and Flakehow. At the village of Mardale Green there was a church, set among yew trees, a vicarage, a school, and the Dun Bull Hotel. The level of the lake was raised 90 ft by the building of a dam 120 ft high and 1,550 ft long, which stretched across the valley below Naddle woods to the bedrock of Burn Banks. Opposition to the scheme had collapsed before the powers of a great and wealthy Corporation finally petered out in 1938. There was a final request that the towering concrete wall of the dam should be darkened to reduce its impact on the scene. Then in the nervous days before the war, Government instructions were given that the dam was to be camouflaged; what was sought on amenity grounds was gained from strategic necessity.

The head of Haweswater from Whiteacre Crag. Harter Fell in the background with the Gatesgarth Pass to Longsleddale to the left and the Nan Bield Pass into Kentmere to the right. Both these routes are ancient bridleways which connect Mardale with Kendal and the southern Lake District. The valley road constructed after the flooding runs along the eastern side of the lake, terminating in a small car-parking area just beyond the belt of trees on the left. A good footpath follows the western shore. The only inhabited building in the catchment area is the hotel, built by Manchester Corporation, which stands lonely above the road in a commanding position about half way along the reservoir. Access on foot in the valley has never been as strictly controlled as at Thirlmere and the absence of afforestation allows the freedom of walking over the fells, about the head of the lake, and to the west. When supplies from Ullswater were brought into the Haweswater complex, treatment became necessary because of the extensive public use of Ullswater and its surroundings. A modern plant was built at Watchgate, north of Kendal, for this purpose. This meant that it became possible to open up Haweswater for more recreation, but the schemes for the provision of picnic sites, caravans and camping, additional car parks, and sailing on the reservoir with a clubhouse and associated activities did not find favour with the Planning Board. Little has been done therefore, apart from the provision of a footpath from Hopgill Beck between the road and the shore to the head of the lake, i.e. to the left in the illustration.

Mardale church about 1920. This stood just below the wooded Rigg a mile beyond the head of the then Hawes Water. The valley road continued beyond the houses at Chapel Hill, opposite the church, with the knoll of Wood Howe on the left (now an island) to Chapel Bridge bearing right to the Dun Bull Inn. The Manchester Bill to authorize the flooding of Mardale was passed by Parliament in 1919 in the face of 76 petitions against it, and work was started in the early 1930s. The church was demolished and its carved windows used in the tower of the intake well at the edge of the reservoir, a little beyond the present hotel. The coffins were removed from the graveyard and buried elsewhere. The intake well is the beginning of the pipeline to Manchester, which passes along a tunnel through the mountains under Selside Pike and Artle Crag into Longsleddale where an aqueduct along the northern side of the valley carries the water to Garnett Bridge to join the pipelines from Thirlmere. On the crest of the lonely moorland between Mardale and Longsleddale there are still two strange stone constructions, widely separated, some 10 ft or so in height, shaped like pairs of upturned binoculars. They were used for the surveying and alignment of the tunnel.

8

Bassenthwaite Lake; across the lake Ullock Pike, and to the right the conical afforested hill of Dod. Skiddaw is in the background. In February 1971 a Cumberland River Authority Bill came before the House of Lords for its second reading. It provided principally for the control of the level of the lake by the building of a weir at its outflow at Ouse Bridge, so that the flow in the River Derwent could be augmented at times of low rainfall and the abstraction of water at the Yearl Weir near Workington by the West Cumberland Water Board could be increased. The height of the weir was to be six in. above the natural level of the lake and maximum draw-down 18 in. below this level. F.L.D. and other bodies petitioned against the Bill but eventually withdrew their objections on the insertion of a clause by which the duration of the powers was to cease on 31 December 1980. By this time the works were to have been demolished and the land reinstated. A number of peers spoke against the Bill, including Lord Birkett, son of a distinguished former President of F.L.D. He said 'it seems to me that while the Bill may be approved it will not be welcome, for it represents, be it ever so small, yet another erosion of the Lake District . . . To the many councils and societies who are dedicated to the preservation of the Lake District it must clearly be discouraging to think that, like so many of our most closely guarded national treasures, it is most often broken into.' The Bill was passed but the Bassenthwaite works have not been carried out, probably because of the time-limit imposed on their duration.

9

The head of Swindale. As wild and lonely a place as any in the eastern fells. The Manchester Corporation Act 1919 empowered the construction of a full-scale dam for a reservoir at the head of Swindale. The dam was to be sited at Truss Gap, but in 1955 the Corporation's engineers decided that it would be sufficient to construct an interception weir at this point to take 12½ million gallons a day. The diverted water would be transferred by buried pipeline and tunnel through the hills of Rosgill Moor and Naddle Forest to Haweswater. This scheme required legal processes for the necessary powers, and a public inquiry was held. There was no objection to the weir but the Lake District Planning Board, F.L.D., and others asked that permission should only be granted if the powers to construct a dam and reservoir were relinquished. This Manchester was reluctant to do. Some months after the inquiry the Minister confirmed the Order to construct the weir, pipeline, and tunnel, but only went so far as to say that there should be an understanding that before proceeding at any time with the construction of Swindale reservoir the Corporation would 'consult with the Lake District Planning Board and the National Park Commission in an endeavour to find some alternative considered to be less harmful to amenity'. Subsequently the Minister received an assurance from Manchester that they would also 'consult with F.L.D. and C.P.R.E.' The powers which remain to construct a reservoir are now vested in the North West Water Authority.

Ullswater from the lake surface in the southern reach with St Sunday Crag in the background. Glenridding is behind the yacht and to the left are the wooded slopes of Keldas, an easily accessible hill providing fine views. A prolonged battle was fought by Manchester Corporation to obtain powers to take water from this lake. The first attempt to secure powers by Parliamentary Bill for this purpose was defeated on its second reading in the House of Lords on 8 February 1962. Lord Birkett, who was closely associated with F.L.D. and other bodies concerned with protection of the countryside, led the opposition to the Bill with great eloquence and skill and secured its defeat. However in January 1965 Manchester Corporation renewed its attack this time seeking a statutory Order to permit abstraction at Gale Bay, near Pooley Bridge, and the transmission of water by tunnel to an underground pumping station near

Parkfoot and so into the Haweswater complex. The Order was the subject of an inquiry in Kendal that summer which lasted 19 days – then considered a prolonged event. The opposition was led by C.P.R.E. and the National Trust supported by a large number of amenity and recreation bodies. About a year later, the Minister of Housing and Local Government accepted the Inspector's recommendation and approved the Order, but with some stringent restrictions and conditions. The most important of these was that, in order to guard against excessive pumping and an unnatural degree of draw-down, the extraction pipe was furnished with a weir placed at such a height that no more water could be drawn when the lake surface had been lowered to 476½ ft, its natural low level. Ullswater is therefore never seen with an exposed sterile rim of stones and mud.

11

Ullswater from the shore footpath through Stybarrow Woods. In a debate in the House of Commons on 27 June 1966 concerning Manchester's water supplies, the late Richard Crossman, then Minister of Housing and Local Government, referred to the work being undertaken by the northern committee of the Water Resources Board in assessing the long-term demands and resources for the whole of the North of England, and concluded by saying 'There will be nothing more from Ullswater. There will be no more artificial reservoirs like the Winster Valley [which had been under discussion as a possible scheme]. There will not be any more of that sort of thing, but we must look forward to the long term. We have to look at the lower reaches of the rivers in this region.'

These assurances were no great comfort when later in 1966 the Ministry of Housing and Local Government issued its report *Cumbrian Rivers: Hydrological Survey* (H.M.S.O.). The introduction disclaimed any intention of judging 'best land use and the preservation of natural beauty' and emphasized that the report was concerned with 'good water

management'. F.L.D. saw here a real threat to the Lake District. 'There can be little doubt', the report stated, 'that more populous and less-watered parts of the country will turn to this area for supplies. Even the external demand is likely to fall short of the potential for many years to come and it follows that development will at first be partial and piece-meal.' 'Here', the report concluded, 'are ample resources for internal needs and a surplus for export to other areas. The problem is to prepare an outline plan of phased development to anticipate ineluctable growth in demand. The early stages will be those whose adverse effects on amenity and land use are least. As need increases and demand rises some concessions will have to be made to ensure the greatest good of the greatest number. At each stage the minimum acceptable flows in the affected rivers must be re-assessed in the light of changing circumstances.'

The Water Resources Board report may well be forgotten, but the words of the Minister in June 1966 should not.

12

Longsleddale from above Wad's Howe. The valley road runs along the foot of the right-hand slopes. The farms on the near side of the valley are linked by a bridleway. Sadgill, the end of the motor road, is at the point where the valley takes a right-hand turn into the rocky defile which leads over the Gatesgarth Pass to Haweswater. Longsleddale, like other cul-de-sac valleys, tends to suffer less from traffic pressure, but it has faced its full measure of threats and miraculously survived. A visitor to the Youth Hostel at Swinklebank in 1939 who comes again today, 40 years later, would see little or no change, except that there is no longer a Youth Hostel there.

In the 1840s, when the route of the railway from Lancaster to Carlisle was being considered, a Kendal Committee urged the choice of a route through Longsleddale by tunnel into Mardale and then along the shores of Haweswater. The advantages of this route were pressed in glowing terms by the Kendal Committee, 'Gatesgarth', they said, 'tapers upwards to a conical point so beautifully that one may almost imagine Nature predestined it for tunnelling'. The Royal Commission appointed for the purpose of determining the route of the line reported that its choice would be closely dictated by the length of the summit tunnel and the nature of the rock through which it would have to be cut. But the Gatesgarth tunnel would have been, for those days, a long and difficult one. So it was thus only an engineering problem, and not amenity reasons, that finally defeated the Longsleddale railway line.

13

14·15

Ennerdale from the track to the site of the former Angler's Inn, now a National Trust car park, The inn, which stood close to the shore, was demolished in the late sixties to prepare for the raising of the lake level, a scheme which has been under discussion for 30 years and more. Ennerdale Water has been used as Whitehaven's water supply since early in the century, but the works there have been modest, and those along the western shore of the lake have now partially disintegrated, become moss-grown, and are screened by shrubs. In 1946, Whitehaven Corporation, then a Water Authority, obtained powers after a public inquiry to raise the lake level by four feet. These works have never been carried out. For when in the sixties the scheme was resurrected, again in the face of opposition, it was found that additional abstractions from the lake were possible without having to raise the level. It would seem that the Anglers' Inn, although then in need of refurbishing, suffered an unnecessary fate. It had long been the haunt of those who loved the peace and tranquillity of Ennerdale and who went there to fish, walk, and climb. In 1977 the scheme to raise the level of the lake was again proposed, now by the North West Water Authority, and partly to meet the needs of British Nuclear Fuels at Windscale. There was widespread opposition to works at Ennerdale which, it was contended, would seriously detract from the natural wildness of this valley.

Ennerdale. Herdus and Bowness Knott seen from the western shore of the lake. Plate 14, the lake at normal level with the water lapping the natural shore line. Plate 15, the level is drawn down about 5 ft exposing extensive areas of mud and stone. This condition, to a greater or lesser degree, has been a regular occurrence over the years during the summer months. It illustrates the damaging effects of draw-down and is a strong argument against the use or increased use of lakes for water supply. In the case of Ennerdale, it has always posed a serious problem as there are extensive shallow areas at the western end of the lake, along the northern shore, and round the head of the lake. Unnatural instability of the water level is also detrimental to shore line aquatic life and vegetation. During the summer of 1978 the water level fell below the outflow into the River Ehen. The Water Authority installed 20 diesel pumps at the weir on the south-western shore of the lake to keep a reasonable flow in the river. The pumps were at work night and day for some weeks. The present scheme to raise the level of Ennerdale Water includes powers to draw down the lake to even lower levels, an overall variation of 11 ft. Although the use of the total range might well be infrequent, it is to conservationists an alarming proposal.

Newby Bridge which spans the River Leven, the outflow of Windermere, a mile or so below the foot of the lake. Manchester Water Order 1966, which authorized abstraction from Windermere, also stated that no water was to be taken from the lake when the flow in the River Leven was less than certain stated amounts; in short, at times of low flow. It also required Manchester Corporation to raise the existing weir (on the far side of the bridge) by six in., or build a new weir six in. higher. Various experiments with scale models were conducted at Manchester University to determine the effect of this work on the lake under various conditions, and the conclusion was reached that it was the bridge that controlled lake levels rather than the design of the weir downstream. It was suggested that flooding could be mitigated by excavating the river bed at and below Newby Bridge itself and that as an additional relief, or as an alternative, a new arch could be added to the bridge on the south side. There were strong objections to interference with, and additions to, this attractive 16th-century bridge. It was contended that the considerable excavations would have endangered the piers. The scheme was abandoned with, up to the present, no disastrous increase in the levels or frequency of floods around Windermere.

In 1976 plans for road alterations to the A590, the Levens Bridge to Barrow-in-Furness road, at Newby Bridge threatened the whole face of this small and highly attractive area. Various schemes were put forward, some versions involving encroachment upon the river and the channel alongside Kid Howe Island on the left in the illustration. The proposals are still under discussion.

17

Flood prevention work, Oxendale Beck, Great Langdale, carried out in the late sixties. Over the years the different drainage authorities have pursued their duties with varying degrees of energy and, in the view of the amenity bodies, sometimes with little concern for scenery and wild life. It was appreciated that measures to protect such valleys as Borrowdale and Langdale from heavy flooding were necessary, but in some cases the becks have been canalised and denuded of vegetation by a level of action well beyond what appeared necessary. River banks reinforced with timber, concrete, and stone, bereft of shrubs, trees, and reeds, afford few habitats for wild life. In 1978 the North West Water Authority was engaged upon a survey of potential drainage-improvement sites and issued a list of 77 areas whose agriculture could benefit from increased arterial drainage. Twenty-three of these 77 sites were wholly or in part designated as being of exceptional importance on account of their wild life, some, such as the Solway marshes, being of Grade I status. Also included in the list were areas of high amenity value such as the head of Bassenthwaite Lake, Kentmere, Mungrisdale, Borrowdale, and Great Langdale.

The Cumbria Naturalists' Trust and others contended that drainage schemes for places of such importance to wild life and to the Cumbrian landscape should be looked at much more carefully than in the past. The cost to amenity and nature conservation must also be weighed in the balance and the true agricultural benefit must be more carefully researched. There should be, it was argued, machinery for public participation in the planning of land-drainage schemes, if necessary by public inquiry.

18

The Wet Sleddale footbridge in its original position.
This ancient bridge would have shared the fate of the
farms of Beckside and Howe, which were drowned
when a dam was built in Wet Sleddale in the early
sixties.

19

The footbridge in Wet Sleddale reconstructed by Manchester Corporation half a mile above the reservoir. The Wet Sleddale reservoir is a small one, although the dam is a considerable construction designed to catch the waters of the valley and feed them into the Haweswater complex. No objection was made to the scheme by any statutory or voluntary body. Care was taken to darken the concrete mass of the east-facing dam which is clearly visible only from the A6 near Shap when water is falling over the spillway, and this it seems to do but rarely. Some tree-planting has been done below the dam and the general concern about amenity and conservation by Manchester Corporation in its last days as a Water Authority is seen here. The rebuilding of the little footbridge, at no more than the expressed wishes of a few individuals, is further evidence of this. Upstream of the bridge, Wet Sleddale remains a wild and primitive place without habitation, where the tumbling rocky beck and the stretches of heather moorland provide the lonely walker with vignettes of beauty.

20

Stott Park Bobbin Mill, Finsthwaite, in 1969, in the last days of its operations. Coppice industries, based in the surrounding woodland have now all but disappeared from the Lake District; only two mills remain, at Spark Bridge, High Furness, and at Staveley, Kendal, the original seat of the industry. One of the buildings at Stott Park was probably a corn-mill before its conversion to bobbin manufacture about 1841. It was water-powered, supplied from the tarn on Finsthwaite Heights which had been enlarged by the mill-owners and is now known as High Dam. High Dam and its surroundings were acquired in 1977 by the Lake District Special Planning Board as an access area.

Whilst the establishments that have been closed in the Lake District were themselves often only small mills or workshops, in total they had an important influence on the growth and prosperity of settlements. The closure of some of the larger establishments such as the ironworks at Backbarrow and bobbin mills in

Staveley and Ambleside in the last 10 to 15 years has been a serious loss to these communities. One of the most significant changes has been the closure of numerous small quarries and mines with the loss of almost 1,000 jobs between 1951 and 1976. The number employed in agriculture also decreased from over 3,600 in 1963 to, 2899 in 1976, but in the greater part of the Lake District agriculture remains an important source of employment. In such places as Satterthwaite, Coniston and Shap, however, forestry and mineral-working are still of predominant importance.

Now only Keswick and Windermere offer a range of job opportunities for the adjoining rural areas, and then on a rather limited scale and mostly associated with tourism. The wider range of jobs and cheaper living available outside the National Park continues to attract young people who seek better working conditions and higher wages than are obtainable in agriculture and forestry.

Ennerdale from Bowness Point. Pillar Mountain (2,927 ft) is right of centre, its lower slopes planted with spruce. The sunlit ridge on the left divides Ennerdale from the Buttermere Valley. Ennerdale, still, remote, and lonely, has been the subject of fierce argument for half a century, firstly because of the afforestation which covers the floor of the valley like an over-large carpet, and secondly because of the proposals for the increased use of its lake for water abstraction. Ennerdale is within the boundaries of the Lake District National Park, so there are added reasons for the protection of its natural beauty. Much of the sitka forest is dark and impenetrable, many of the paths give only occasional glimpses to the wider scenes of this dramatic dale, but the hardy walker can still climb above the trees to a tough and unfrequented terrain.

The Forestry Commission has plans to improve the appearance of the Ennerdale forests by breaking up the hard outer lines of the planting, by selective felling, and by the introduction of different species. These schemes are being worked out with the expert advice of landscape architects and will be the subject of consultation with the planning authority and other interested bodies. The forestry access road, prohibited to public vehicular use, is on the left. By-laws which apply to this restriction are not merely academic but have been enforced on occasions. The Commission takes the illegal use of the road seriously and the general policy of restricting intrusion of the motor car into remote places must be supported.

22

Pillar Mountain from High Stile on the ridge between Ennerdale and Buttermere. Pillar Rock, famous for its rock climbs, rises above the shadowed combe. The regimented ranks of spruce cover the valley floor and the forest tracks stand out prominently. The ancient bridleway along the dale runs on the right bank of the River Liza and just out of view. This particular afforestation was much criticized in the thirties and it was successfully urged that planting of this type should not be carried out elsewhere in the Lake District. It was rightly contended by H. H. Symonds that not only did it cause a high degree of damage to natural beauty but imposed severe restrictions on freedom of access to the hills. Before the planting, a walker could take the bridleway into Ennerdale and leave the track where he wished, to climb the slopes to either ridge. But following the acquisition of land by the Commission and fencing with sheep-proof wire netting topped with barbed wire, the freedom was

gone. Once planting had taken place the walker could no longer take cross-country routes and was confined to the paths provided. In his book *Afforestation in the Lake District* (1936) Symonds pointed out that when the Commission's property was entered through a gate in the fencing at the western end, there was a notice which stated 'To the Pillar – Please Keep to the Roadway', and another forbidding the use of an inviting bridge over the River Liza.

23

Pillar Mountain from the track through Ennerdale forest. In 1936 when disagreement raged about the planting of conifers in the Lake District the Forestry Commission wrote in their defence, 'An accurate comparison would be with alpine forests in which the trees are seen against a background of higher country'. This comparison was quickly challenged – the scale of the English Lake District, it was pointed out, is quite different to that of the Alps, and its small and intimate beauty was so much more delicate and easily damaged. 'Recall Ennerdale', Symonds wrote in 1936 in *Afforestation in the Lake District*, 'From the summit of Pillar range the fells drop without a pause to the valley bottom. Trigonometry gives the net rise as a mere 2,200 ft, but the canons of beauty are negligent of this arithmetic; in Nature's architecture, which has another scale, the Pillar range stands up in stupendous command. And the grandeur is an effect of contrasts, of bare slope in the lower contours and a serrated skyline of the volcanic rock above; in between is steep, broken crag, set among the colours of the fell side; here and there a vertical stream bed, or a fan of scree spilled into the grass and bracken of the lower, horizontal slopes, pulls the wide extension of the valley bottom into unity with the crag and steepness far above; there is a great composition. – This is Ennerdale as it was. Now draw across these lower contours a continuous forest in one continuous colour, and that a dull colour. The unbroken horizontal line of the tree belt, drab in itself and blotting out all the delicate ground work, brings down the whole scale of Nature's composition and mishandles its proportions. For you are not operating in the Alps; you have not the depth and distance.' The same forest, he said, might be all right in Bedfordshire or on the long slopes of the Pennines, but in Ennerdale, austere and primitive and noble as any piece of England, all taste and discretion should have said 'elsewhere'.

24

The Duddon Valley from the lower slopes of Harter Fell. The area of the 1936 Forestry Agreement did not include the farmlands of Black Hall at the head of the Duddon and Brotherilkeld at the head of Eskdale, but in 1943, under pressure from the amenity organizations, especially F.L.D., the Forestry Commission entered into a covenant with the National Trust agreeing not to plant the Brotherilkeld land. Planting in the Duddon Valley was started just before the Second World War around Birks Farm, now hidden in trees, and continued along the flanks of Harter Fell and along the craggy western side of the river southwards. There was consultation as the work proceeded between the Forestry Commission and representatives of the National Trust and F.L.D. The more acceptable results of these discussions are evident today when this planting is compared with the planting on the Whinlatter Pass and in Ennerdale. As the work of planting moved northwards towards the great bowl in which the Duddon is joined by Cockley Beck, there was a firm stand by the amenity bodies against any further afforestation. In 1958 an agreement was reached under which the Forestry Commission surrendered all plans to plant on any part of Brotherilkeld and Black Hall. A price was fixed at which these two hill farms were acquired by the National Trust, under whose ownership traditional fell-farming continues today.

25 Upper Eskdale. The valley road to the foot of the
Hardknott Pass bears away to the right across the
picture. The conical peak in the background is Bow
Fell. In 1935 the Forestry Commission bought 7,000
acres in Eskdale and Dunnerdale with which it
intended to create the Hardknott Forest Park. The area
to be planted included the right-hand side of the

valley, as seen in this illustration, to the slopes above Brotherilkeld farm beyond the Hardknott road. There were strong objections to the proposed afforestation. One scheme that the Forestry Commission suggested was to leave 440 acres in Eskdale unplanted on payment by public subscription of compensation money to the Forestry Commission. F.L.D. would not support this compromise and held the opinion that there should be no planting at all in Eskdale and Dunnerdale. The Society proceeded to organize a petition pressing the point on the Commission and urging that there should be no further planting of the Whinlatter and Ennerdale kind in what must be 'an inviolate national heritage'.

26

Gill Bank above Boot in Eskdale, one of the seven farms given to the National Trust in 1977 by Lake District Farm Estates. Farm Estates was formed in 1937, at a time when the National Trust was much less strong, to acquire farms with the declared purpose of maintaining traditional farming and preserving traditional Lake District buildings. The Company was closely associated with F.L.D. which at various times gave financial support to it as well as having a number of members common to both executive committees. Over the years Farm Estates bought a number of properties in the Lake District, within 20 miles of the Langdale Pikes. Among the original sponsors were such famous Lake District defenders as the late Lords Birkett and Chorley, F. C. Scott of the Kendal-based Provincial Insurance Company, and the Rev. H. H. Symonds, founder of the F.L.D. The Company was also linked closely with the National Trust. The rules provided that all property acquired must be placed under covenant to the Trust, protecting it against development and unsightly exploitation, and that any farm to be sold must be offered first to the National Trust. In the early seventies it became increasingly difficult to pay for the essential maintenance of the farms out of income and even more difficult to carry out improvements. It was decided that the basic purposes of Farm Estates would best be achieved by giving the farms, which had vastly increased in value, to the National Trust. The Company has now been finally wound up.

The gift to the National Trust was one of the largest and most important since the Second World War and the farms, beside being of great amenity value, added to and in some cases also adjoined the Trust's large holdings in the Lake District. As well as Gill Bank the farms in the gift were Yew Tree Farm in Borrowdale, Mireside on the shores of Ennerdale Water, Ghyll and Harrowhead close under the crags of Buckbarrow in Wasdale, Howe Green, the white-washed farmhouse which is in the centre of the attractive hamlet of Hartsop, and High Nook, Loweswater.

27

Borrowdale from above Manesty. Grange can be seen situated on the almost flat valley floor at the edge of the pasture with the wooded slopes beyond rising to King's How. The dark hill on the right is Castle Crag. This part of Borrowdale and the environs of Derwent Water have the greatest concentration of broadleaved woods in the north of the Lake District. From Lodore southwards, on the far side of the valley in this illustration, the steep valley sides, covered in trees, provide some of the finest woodland landscapes in the National Park. They are of international importance with rich Atlantic flora, and are described in *A Nature Conservation Review* (by D. A. Ratcliffe, 2 vols. 1977) as being, as a group, in the first echelon of Grade I sites.

Virtually all the woodland is growing on the site of former forests which were exploited for timber and charcoal during earlier centuries, but with natural regeneration and replanting with native trees they approach in character the original natural woodland of the district.

Most of this woodland is owned by the National Trust which has entered into dedication agreements with the Forestry Commission. The agreements aim at the management of woodland for timber production. There has been criticism in some quarters that management should be more specifically for nature-conservation purposes; then, generally speaking, its landscape value would also be maintained.

28

Tree-planting ceremony at Bowness-on-Windermere. Over the years tree-planting, as opposed to afforestation, has received encouragement and support from the planning authorities and the conservation bodies. The National Trust has carried out a good deal of amenity planting, often receiving gifts for this purpose from members. In recent years the National Park authority and the County Councils have given grants for tree-planting, and money is also available for this purpose from the Countryside Commission. Finding sites for planting, especially for large trees to make a material contribution to the landscape, is not easy. Such bodies as the National Trust, owning extensive lands, find the task simpler than do say the Women's Institutes who are nevertheless eager to take part in the various campaigns to promote tree-planting.

European Conservation Year was commemorated in 1970, when F.L.D. provided a limited amount of finance for planting schemes by Women's Institutes and other bodies. Planting took place, usually with modest ceremony, at Colby near Appleby, Long Marton, Knock, Kirkby Thore, Winton near Kirkby Stephen, Urswick, Mill Moss, Patterdale, Holme, Staveley, Natland near Kendal, and at Outgate near Ambleside. The 'Plant a Tree in '73 Campaign' brought a new stimulus to planting and there were Exchequer grants for local authority schemes. Unfortunately these were not taken up to any great extent.

29

The Rusland Beeches. In 1953 the Planning Board made these mature beech trees, which number more than a hundred, the subject of a Tree Preservation Order. This prohibited the felling of the trees except with the permission of the Board and upon such conditions as they might impose. In 1956 the land upon which the beeches stood was offered on a long lease to the Forestry Commission, together with a large acreage of adjoining land on the slopes above the trees, for the Commission to include in its local programme of afforestation. The effect of granting such a lease would have been that the Tree Preservation Order would then cease to have any legal force and the Commission could if it wished fell the trees or allow the owner to do so. It was in fact a condition of the proposed lease with the Commission that the trees should be felled by the owner. The Planning Board was consulted and expressed its strong objection. At this point F.L.D. intervened, making representations directly to the owner to take over the trees and be responsible for their maintenance. The owner withdrew his offer of a lease to the Forestry Commission and granted a 50 years' lease of the trees, and a strip of land 75 yds wide alongside them, to F.L.D. trustees who commissioned an expert survey. It was found necessary to fell a few of the trees and others were lopped and treated in various ways. Some replanting was carried out and other replacements have since been made as occasion arises. Access remains open, providing among the smooth boles of the great trees delightful picnic places, in autumn on a russet carpet of leaves and in spring under a canopy of shimmering green. In 1976 the lease was transferred to the Planning Board on the understanding that the Board would care for and protect the trees in the same way as F.L.D. had done in the previous 20 years.

30

Martindale from the slopes of Hallin Fell, with Beda Fell in the centre. This remote and unspoiled complex of dales is reached from Pooley Bridge by the narrow road to Howtown and then by the steep hill over Martindale Hause. There are innumerable and highly attractive ways on foot in the valleys and along the ridges. Martindale too has been a battleground – literally, and not only for conservation issues. Three thousand acres of this area were, during the Second World War, used as a field firing-range. In 1946 F.L.D. took the first steps in asking the War Department to surrender this area and in stimulating protests in the press against the Army's occupation. The process of regaining the freedom of Martindale was a slow and complicated one; the clearing of unexploded shells alone took two years. The War Department's attitude was that it would only give up Martindale if a suitable alternative area could be provided not too far distant. Part of the northern Howgills was agreed upon, but eventually, in the face of Government economies, this was not pursued and Martindale was finally released.

There was further trouble in 1951 when a public inquiry was held concerning the electricity supply to three farms in Martindale. Whilst an overhead line was chosen, its route was modified. The action of the amenity groups did much to preserve the appearance of a lonely area.

31

Thirlmere – nature trail at Launchy Gill. In the early 1960s there was much controversy about the restrictions on public access in the Thirlmere Valley. The public enjoyment of a valley close to the centre of the National Park was severely limited and there was widespread criticism of the ubiquitous notices, in red lettering, that declared trespassers would be prosecuted. The Water Authority contended that little could be done to remedy the situation as no facilities existed to treat and purify the Thirlmere water should it suffer contamination from the public use of the catchment area. The strictest conditions applied, and apply, to the few people permitted to fish in the lake. However, some concessions were granted. Increased provision was made for car parking – up to the mid sixties it had been difficult to find a place to leave a car even if one wished to walk a public right-of-way, say from Armboth to Watendlath. Two nature trails were established; one at Swirls starting near the Station Coppice lay-by at the northern end of the lake, the other, more interesting one, at Launchy Gill on the western side. In addition a path has been made from Dunmail Raise through the forest to Thirlspot, a useful route for walkers as an alternative in bad weather to the ridge of Helvellyn. There is still no public access to the shore of the lake, and the encircling roads are walled off and topped with wire. Thirlmere's water is probably the purest source in the north-west and up to the present its treatment before distribution has been minimal. Before extending public access and the use of the lake for sailing and other activities a proper treatment plant would be necessary. The Water Authority had a scheme to provide this, and the works are now under construction. Even so, it seems now that the planning authorities and certainly the conservation bodies would be opposed to any but the most discreet opening up of this valley. Increased access on foot around the lake and in other parts of the catchment area, with the modification of walls and fences, will probably be the full extent of future works.

The Hardknott Pass near the summit on the Eskdale side. This pass is more taxing than the Wrynose Pass, being steeper and more circuitous. There are discouraging notices warning of steep gradients. The road is frequently blocked by vehicles failing on sections with especially severe gradients. As with the Wrynose Pass, and with the Blea Tarn road between Great and Little Langdale, it has long been contended that there should be some control over usage. One-way systems, or tidal flow westwards in the morning and eastwards in the afternoon, seem too complicated and to require too much supervision. Closure to the motor car at busy times has been advocated. The distances involved are small; the Wrynose Pass from Little Langdale to Cockley Beck is four miles, the Hardknott Pass from Cockley Beck to the head of Eskdale two and a half miles, and the Blea Tarn road from Little Langdale to Dungheon Ghyll three miles. In the absence of cars these roads would be good footpaths. At present their overburdened state in the season makes their use unpleasant, frustrating and dangerous. It is impossible to appreciate this splendid countryside from a seat in a car. The closure of the passes at peak periods would also have benefit by relieving traffic pressures on the narrow roads of Eskdale, the Duddon, and the Langdales, as these would become cul-de-sac valleys. These more firm and positive forms of traffic management to protect the mountainous heart of the National Park have long been advocated by F.L.D.

33

The A591 at Lowwood on the shores of Windermere with the Langdale Pikes in the background. This road runs from Kendal through the heart of the National Park by Windermere, Ambleside, Grasmere, and Keswick and then northwards along the eastern side of Bassenthwaite Lake to Bothel where it joins the A595. It passes through scenery of the highest quality, skirting the northern reaches of Windermere, and then by Rydal Water and Grasmere, Thirlmere, and Bassenthwaite Lake. On its descent into Keswick it gives fine views into Borrowdale and across to the mountains which contain the Newlands Valley and the Whinlatter Pass. It is one of this country's most scenic roads. From its earliest reports on traffic in the 1930s, F.L.D. contended that in any alterations to this road precedence should be given to environmental considerations; that traffic pressure should give way to the preservation of the natural scene.

Over the years the road has been 'improved' almost along its whole length and fears that a major upgrading would push further and further into the Park have often been expressed. The linking of the M6 with the Kendal western bypass by a dual carriageway has made it possible for vehicles to reach the boundary of the Park at speeds which need not be relaxed from the Midlands and other large centres of population; speeds that are inappropriate in the Park itself. Further dualling of the A591, although considered and planned by the highway authority, has been resisted by the Planning Board and the amenity bodies.

Traffic impasse at the foot of the Wrynose Pass, Little Langdale, on a holiday weekend. Such situations are not infrequent on summer weekends. The chaos usually has to be untangled without police intervention. A motorist with initiative and a sense of leadership takes control and the cars are dispersed, only for a similar situation to arise again here or elsewhere on the narrow twisting steep road. The road through Little Langdale is a typical lakeland dale road, closely walled, first running through woodland above the infant Brathay then through the scattered hamlet and on, edging its way around rocky knolls and field corners; a road with a delightful setting and superb views which has evolved slowly from some ancient trackway. It has remained almost unchanged this century. But it cannot cope with the modern car in the numbers that now seek to use it. At the beginning of the Little Langdale road at Colwith Bridge there is a discouraging notice warning of steep gradients and of the possibility of long delays. This seems to be largely ignored.

Various solutions to the traffic problem have been suggested. The road surface might be allowed to deteriorate, which it would do with rapidity, providing a more effective discouragement than notice boards. This solution is not considered acceptable, particularly by the highway authorities. Road widening, or the extensive provision of passing places, would be obtrusive and unsuitable in this mountainous terrain. The proper solution put forward a number of years ago by F.L.D. and advocated on many occasions since, is the closure of the pass to cars at peak periods and the provision of a mini-bus service. The 'Mountain Goat' mini-bus service already travels this route.

35·36

The A591 on the southern side of Dunmail Raise before and after reconstruction. The straightening, and widening to three lanes, of the road on the then Westmorland side of the pass was carried out in 1971, with a section of dual carriageway over the summit itself. This dualling was criticized by F.L.D. as damaging to the landscape and destructive of more of the open common land than was strictly necessary. The highway authority justified the design by claiming that a dual carriageway, on different levels to fit the contours of the land, was preferable to a wider road that would require cuttings and embankments. The divided carriageways would also leave undisturbed the large ancient cairn reputed to be the burial place of King Dunmail. So today the remains of this former King of Cumbria may still lie beneath the cairn, but hardly in peace.

In recent years the top of Dunmail Raise has acquired something of the sterility of a motorway. The open common has of necessity been fenced off to stop the slaughter of sheep by fast-moving traffic. Little provision has been made for parking and those who wish to go into the mountains from this point receive scant encouragement to do so. Immediately over the summit of the pass the road changes abruptly and remains unaltered, except for kerbing and marking, all along the shore of Thirlmere.

37

White Moss Common with Rydal Water on the right.
This is the heart of Wordsworth country with crag,
lake, oaks, silver birch, and mossy rock. Wordsworth's
Grasmere cottage is less than a mile away and Rydal
Mount, his home 1813–50, is among the trees in the
middle distance. The A591 runs across the picture to
the edge of the lake. This too is an area heavily used
by the tourist. The Common is owned by the National
Trust which, with the Lake District Special Planning
Board, has prepared a management plan that includes
careful provision for car parking. Formerly cars were
parked haphazardly over the whole of the foreground
area and on summer days even along the bank of the
river, excluding the less fortunate and impeding the
water play of the young. There is now only access to
this area on foot. Space for cars has been made among
the dense birch, and across the road to the left in an
extensive old quarry where the Planning Board has
tidied the site, constructed earth embankments to
break up the mass of cars, and planted a large number
of trees. White Moss Common is a good example of
the successful management of a small, highly
attractive area, subjected to heavy pressure from
visitors. Opinions differed as to what facilities should
be provided and about how far they should be
allowed to obtrude; for instance, public conveniences
were accepted as a necessity, but deciding on a site for
them involved endless argument. Café and other
refreshment provision was thought to be out of place,
and is in any case available in nearly every village and
town.

38

Work in progress on the A591 at Shoulthwaite north of Thirlmere in the early 1960s. The undulating old road was left as the southbound carriageway, while this rock-cutting takes the northbound carriageway into a length of three-lane highway before returning to the substantially unchanged road at Dalebottom. From here to Keswick there has been little alteration. Travelling in the sixties from Kendal to Keswick through sections where roadworks were in progress on a considerable scale, one gained the impression that it was the intention of the highway authorities to upgrade the road to a fast through route. Plans existed to dual, widen, and straighten other lengths of the road, but they have not been carried out and now, in the light of new thinking about roads in National Parks, seem far less likely ever to be implemented. There has been continual pressure to keep heavy vehicles whose origin and destination are outside the National Park, i.e. those vehicles travelling between the South and west Cumbria, off the A591. These vehicles, which contribute substantially to the traffic difficulties of Ambleside and on the twisting and undulating sections of the A591, should now be routed by the M6 motorway and the reconstructed A66. Some road-transport operators are already using this route, particularly in the tourist season, but it is intended to prohibit through heavy goods vehicles using the A591 by a Traffic Order – a move advocated by F.L.D. for many years.

The A591 on the shores of Windermere. The battle to take through heavy goods vehicles off this road goes back to the mid 1930s. In 1937 F.L.D. was investigating the effects of increased traffic on the Lake District. It was looking forward to the improvement of the main A6 (Kendal–Shap–Carlisle) route, for which the highway authorities planned to build a viaduct at Huck's Bridge to span the deep valley of the Borrowbeck as well as carry out other upgrading work. F.L.D. thought this would result in more commercial vehicles using this route rather than the Windermere–Rydal–Dunmail Raise road (A591) and so there would be 'neither need nor temptation further to commercialize and widen the most beautiful piece of road in England'. Also in 1937 an F.L.D. deputation went to the Cumberland County Council to object to the 'improvement' of the road over Newlands Hause to Buttermere. 'The pleasant lane between hedgerows gives place at Keskadale, where it begins

to run across the steep slope of the open fellside, to a wide tarmac road cut well into the hill on one side and supported on the other by a quite considerable embankment.' There was, the Society complained, now an equally regrettable new motor road on Honister; 'Where the walker had happiness for his feet and eyes there is now an intractable mileage of tarmac and a positive circus course for motors – a triangle from Keswick by the Honister Pass to Buttermere and so from Buttermere by Newlands Hause back to Keswick.' The policy must be, said F.L.D., to provide good approach roads to the Lake District, a sound peripheral ring road, but no motorization of the dalehead or of the still virgin passes.

A kind of opinion poll was organized which invited signatures to a statement against indiscriminate road improvements. Eleven thousand people signed, of whom rather more than a third declared themselves to be owners or drivers of cars.

40

A592 on the Kirkstone Pass. The road climbs from the Troutbeck Valley and takes a declivity in the hills between Red Screes in the background and St Raven's Edge. This road has not changed in width and alignment this century. It is closely bounded by stone walls. In summer time it is heavily trafficked and much used by motor-coach tour operators. There is parking provision at the Kirkstone Inn on the summit for approximately 70 cars, which at most times of year is sufficient. There is a heavier demand, and a varying degree of chaos, when a snowfall brings conditions suitable for skiing. Yellow lines have been painted along extensive stretches of the road on both sides of the summit in recent years to prevent prolonged jams. In the *Report on Traffic in the Lake District National Park* prepared jointly by the County Surveyors and Planning Officers of the then three Counties of Lancashire, Westmorland, and Cumberland in 1965 it was visualized that by 1974 parking provision would be required at the summit of the Kirkstone Pass for 700 cars. Fortunately this has not been necessary nor does it seem likely to be. H. Wilson and J. L. Womersley in their *Traffic Management in the Lake District National Park* of 1972 considered the road over the Kirkstone Pass to be unsuitable for large buses and coaches, which frequently caused hold-ups and blockages because of their difficulty in passing vehicles, in particular each other. It was recommended that this traffic on the Pass should be limited to mini-buses. In recent times this type of restriction has been proposed by the highway authority and consultations on these issues are under way.

St. John's Vale and the Helvellyn range from the slopes of Lonscale Fell before the reconstruction of the A66. The wooded gorge of the River Greta runs across the picture. The route of the then A66, screened by its walls and hedges, is not visible. Twenty-three miles of the A66 are in the National Park and it was argued in the late sixties and at the A66 Public inquiry in 1972 that it would be wrong to upgrade this road to a major highway linking the M6 at Penrith with industrial west Cumberland. The scale of the proposed reconstruction, with the size of the major engineering works, roundabouts, and embankments and cuttings, was out of keeping with the scenery of the Lake District. The alternative proposal submitted by the objectors was for the use of the improved B5305 (linked with the M6 at the Catterlen interchange) and the A595 – a route less undulating, at a lower level, but admittedly four miles longer. This distance was not significant in the lengthy journeys of most vehicles and was not, in the opinion of the Inquiry Inspector, considered to be of consequence. The alternative route included one major problem; crossing the valley of the River Caldew at Sebergham; but against this had to be weighed the expensive crossing of the Greta Gorge at Keswick and a number of other bridging operations and large engineering structures on the A66.

42

The Greta Bridge under construction in 1974. This bridge, on the Keswick northern bypass section of the A66, carries the road, a dual two-lane carriageway, over Greta Gorge. The bridge is 110 ft above the river and is 720 ft long. It is by far the largest concrete construction in the Lake District and is in a particularly beautiful part of the National Park. In spite of the care taken in its design, its impact is unavoidably great. As a consequence of considerable engineering difficulties in the foundations of the piers and anchoring the bridge platform on the unstable Skiddaw slates on the northern side of the structure, the financial cost of the scheme was much greater than anticipated. The Inquiry Inspector in his report had acknowledged that some structures on the A66 would 'permanently dominate' the scene, and this viaduct is certainly one of them.

43

The A66 under construction on the shores of Bassenthwaite Lake. This is the eastbound carriageway of a dualled road, the former A66 carrying the westbound traffic. In the background are Skiddaw and Ullock Pike. The road was constructed along the line of the former Keswick to Workington railway, but much exceeded its single-track width. It made new encroachment on the lake, in places by as much as 90 ft. The building of the new road along the shore of Bassenthwaite Lake was considered by the objectors to the A66 reconstruction to be a particularly damaging part of the scheme. Traffic now travels the long straight stretches of the new road at speeds so high that the views across the lake can only be glimpsed

momentarily, and usually with heavy goods vehicles in the foreground. Sections have proved to be fatally dangerous. The Inquiry Inspector did recommend that the design should be modified, to reduce encroachment into the lake and to reduce the design speed to 50 m.p.h., but these points were not accepted by the Secretary of State. Much was made by the promoters of the A66 scheme of the provision of a footpath along the lake side of the road and preparatory work for it can be seen in the photograph. It is rarely used. The traffic noise and fumes override the peace and beauty of the lake and the path has little appeal to walkers.

44

The A66 north of Keswick sweeping over the flat land between Derwent Water and Bassenthwaite Lake, with Grisedale Pike in the background. The forests of the Whinlatter can be seen on the right. The roundabout is the intersection of the A66 and the A591, the latter of which runs on the eastern side of Bassenthwaite Lake. An earlier section of new road, the Portinscale bypass, is left of centre. The design speed of 60 m.p.h. imposes certain standards of horizontal and vertical alignment which are inappropriate in the landscape of the Lake District National Park. Although after a prolonged public inquiry in the early months of 1972 the Secretary of State for the Environment gave permission for the scheme to go ahead, there were grave and widespread misgivings. Subsequent government pronouncements have declared that 'investment in trunk roads should be directed to developing routes for long-distance traffic which avoid National Parks', and that 'no new route for long-distance traffic should be constructed through a National Park, or existing road upgraded, unless it has been demonstrated that there is a compelling need which would not be met by any reasonable alternative means.' (D.o.E., Circular 4/76.)

45

The mass walk to the summit of Latrigg, Keswick, on 14 October, 1973. The demonstration, in which a thousand people took part, was organized by F.L.D. to show the continuing opposition to the construction of a major road through the Lake District. The photograph was taken during a pause in the walk for looking at the line of the Keswick bypass section of the A66 which was planned to run between the slopes of the hill and the nearest houses of Keswick. The summit of Latrigg was reached a little before 3 p.m. A cold wind was blowing under a heavily clouded sky and the crowd settled a little below the ridge on the leeward side. The speeches were brief. Roland Wade, Chairman of F.L.D., read a message from Lord Hunt, who had written to say how much he regretted not being present to join old personal friends and 'all others who are friends of the Lake District' in the protest about the Minister's A66 decision. 'It is necessary to warn the Government', he said, 'of growing concern about action which promotes material expediency in preference to environmental values. It is a deplorable business. Let there be no more such Governmental errors of judgment in the Lake District'. Gerald Haythornthwaite, Chairman of the Standing Committee on National Parks (now the Council for National Parks), spoke next and referred to the scene of mountain, dale, and lake which was spread before the meeting. 'These riches', he said, 'are beyond price and belong to all mankind of this and following generations. They are not to be traded for any transient commercial advantage nor are they to be degraded to provide unlimited access and high-speed procession for motor-borne visitors. Yet this is what the Government intends by the approval of the Order. . . . Every viaduct, traffic exchange, embankment, and cutting which would divorce the road from the topography of the land mocks its nature and derides its beauty'.

A resolution was put to and passed by the assembly with no hand or voice raised against, that 'This meeting on the summit of Latrigg deplores the decision of the Secretary of State for the Environment to approve the proposals for massive development of the A66 which would do irreparable damage to the Lake District landscape and destroy the essential qualities and character of this part of the National Park. The meeting urges the Secretary of State to hold up the construction of the road so that the much less damaging schemes already designed may be adopted. These provide for a more modest bypass of Keswick and the diversion of heavy traffic to a route outside the National Park. Let it not be said by future generations that the Government threw away this last chance to prevent a major disaster to the Lake District National Park'.

Illustration reproduced by the kind permission of the copyright-holder Ivor Nicholas

46

The A66, Keswick bypass section. Here a three-lane highway crosses the lower slopes of Latrigg. Keswick lies to the right, in the distance the Dodds, the northern end of the Helvellyn range. The illustration is from Spooney Green bridge on the walkers' route from Keswick by Latrigg to Skiddaw. In the distance Brundholme bridge, a considerable construction aslant the new highway which carries the little road that twists through the woods to Brundholme farm. And beyond this bridge the new highway crosses the River Greta. This huge road is rarely heavily congested; indeed it is frequently seen without vehicles. The Secretary of State conceded that the traffic would not justify the expenditure by the then standards of economic return.

The question of a bypass for Keswick, now incorporated into the overall upgrading of the A66, had long been a subject of discussion. In the 1960s a southern bypass of Keswick was considered, a scheme which would have divided the town from the lake. In the face of much objection this route was abandoned. It was generally accepted that Keswick needed the relief of a bypass but it was contended by the Planning Board, the Countryside Commission, F.L.D., and others that a more modest scheme, following closely the line of the disused railway, would have been more acceptable and more effective than the A66 solution.

47

The site of the A66 Keswick interchange in 1969 seen from the slopes of Latrigg. The then A66 immediately east of Keswick runs across the lower part of the picture with the now-demolished Briery Cottages on the extreme left. The Helvellyn range is in the distance, and Great How, at the foot of Thirlmere, conical and tree-covered, is beyond the sunlit fields in the centre.

48

The same site in 1976 prior to the completion of the Greta bridge in the bottom right-hand corner. The tree-lined road running above the interchange leads to Castlerigg Stone Circle and remains unchanged.

49

The Kent Estuary from Arnside Knott. The viaduct carries the Carnforth to Barrow-in-Furness railway. Across the estuary are the mosses of Meathop and to the right the limestone ridge of Whitbarrow. In the late 1960s a scheme was proposed for an entirely new road of eight and a half miles to link the A6 near Yealand Redmayne to the A590 (the Levens–Barrow road) near Lindale. The road was planned to cross the estuary just north, i.e. on the far side, of the railway viaduct on a massive 13-span bridge. Between the A6 and the estuary the road was to cross unspoiled and highly attractive countryside through cuttings ploughed up to 24 ft deep and across extensive embankments. Ironically, at this same time the Countryside Commission planned to designate this area as an Area of Outstanding Natural Beauty. A Committee was formed to co-ordinate the voluntary societies and various other interests that were opposed to the road scheme, and in the first instance this Committee exerted pressure for a public inquiry. It was granted by the Secretary of State for the Environment and took place at Grange-over-Sands in 1971. The Objection Committee's costs for legal representations, engineering consultants, and witnesses exceeded £3,000. Over two years later the Secretary of State announced his decision against the Arnside Link road. The Arnside-Silverdale area has since received the official designation as an Area of Outstanding Natural Beauty.

50

The bypass of Lindale on the A590 Levens Bridge to Barrow-in-Furness road. This was opened in 1976 and is part of the upgrading of the whole length of the Barrow road. The old road through Lindale village was a difficult and dangerous one on a steep gradient. Major new sections of the road have been completed at Backbarrow and Haverthwaite, and others are planned at Levens Bridge, across the whole length at Meathop Moss, at High Newton, Newby Bridge, Greenodd, and Dalton. F.L.D. in its earliest statement of traffic policy (1939) had advocated that the peripheral roads of the Lake District should be upgraded and that the internal roads should be retained in their existing character. The Barrow road was one that was recognized as demanding improvement. It is doubtful whether it was realized then on what a large scale the new road would be constructed. In recent years F.L.D. has criticized the devastating magnitude of the plans for certain sections of this road, in particular for the Levens Bridge bypass and at High Newton and Newby Bridge. At the same time it should be remembered that at the Arnside Link road inquiry the objectors' case was that the proper solution for improving access to Barrow was not a new link to the A6 but a dualling of the existing Levens–Lindale road. This submission was accepted by the Secretary of State.

51

The Borrowbeck Viaduct on the M6 motorway under construction in 1968. On both sides of the bridge are the huge pre-cast concrete beams for the decking. The view is northwards towards Tebay. The River Lune is tree-lined to the right. Close beside the motorway is the main London (Euston) to Glasgow railway line. The road to the left, A685 Kendal-Tebay, was realigned on a new bridge. The Borrowbeck runs away to the left and its valley is one under investigation by the North West Water Authority for use as a new reservoir.

The M6 motorway runs along the eastern side of the Lake District National Park, only entering it for about half a mile in Lowther Park. It passes through highly scenic countryside between the Farleton and Penrith interchanges. The choice of this route through the uplands about Killington and the Lune Gorge followed careful studies. The Consulting Engineers, Scott, Wilson, Kirkpatrick, & Partners, had special concern for the natural beauty of the countryside, employing in their design divided carriageways where it was considered that the impact would be reduced or agriculture would benefit, and stepped carriageways where the contoured hillside more readily accommodated this type of construction. But the road with its many bridges, embankments, cuttings, and other structures, was a vast engineering undertaking which could not be carried out without changing the countryside through which it was to run. There is now a noise band of at least two miles, its extent determined by the wind and the nature of intervening terrain. The ceaseless roar of traffic can be heard from the summits of the Howgill Fells and from the Whinfell range. However, the necessity for the M6 was generally accepted. There was little objection except from individual landowners and no public inquiry was held.

The completed M6 motorway in the Lune Gorge, looking southwards from Jeffrey's Mount, showing the Borrowbeck viaduct and, to the right, the A685 Kendal-Tebay road. A section of the former Kendal road can also be seen close to the River Lune beyond the motorway. Alternative routes for the motorway were investigated. Some followed a direct line near Kendal and the A6, but then had to negotiate the mountains to the north. Others, going about six miles to the east, went through the Lune Gorge near the route of the railway. The A6 group had a number of variations but involved tunnelling for one and a half miles under the summit of Shap Fells. This made the capital cost of the route appreciably higher but being some two and a half miles shorter traffic-operating costs would be less. Weather conditions, which for the first time for a motorway scheme were carefully studied, played a part in the selection of the route. The Killington-Tebay route proved to be less susceptible to low cloud although there was little choice when considering the effects of snow and ice. There were objections to a tunnel because it would require a permanent organization for its maintenance and operation, because of the absence of continuous hard shoulders, and because of possible restrictions on the passage of vehicles carrying dangerous loads. So finally the Lune Gorge route was chosen.

The Minister of Transport declared the road open on 23 October 1970. It may well be contended that to some extent the motorway has acted as a great bypass for the Lake District. Heavy goods vehicles to and from west Cumbria, which formerly used the A591 through the heart of the Lake District, now take the M6 and A66. Many tourists from the South find the motorway induces them to drive onwards to the Lowlands and Highlands of Scotland, when formerly they would have found the Lake District far enough.

53

The head of Longsleddale showing the track from Sadgill to the Gatesgarth Pass. Goat Scar on the left and Buckbarrow Crag on the right. Beyond Goat Scar the main tributary of the River Sprint, Wren Gill, comes from the west and here there are the considerable tips and workings of slate quarries, long abandoned. In 1947 there was for a time a vigorously pursued scheme to reopen the quarries and install an aerial ropeway on steel pylons for the one and a half miles to Sadgill. Such a proposal would have ruined not only the wild head of the dale, but have completely changed the whole character of Longsleddale. The scheme came to nothing. In the early 1960s when a route was being investigated for the extension northwards of the M6 motorway from Carnforth, the possibility of taking this great highway up Longsleddale and by tunnel beneath the Gatesgarth Pass was considered. This time the scheme was abandoned, not on account of engineering difficulties, for modern equipment and techniques would have made light work of a two-mile tunnel, but rather because it was realized that there would be great opposition to such a highway within the National Park.

In 1964 Manchester Corporation sought to include in the Ullswater and Windermere Water Order powers to construct a duplicate tunnel and pipeline from Haweswater along the floor of Longsleddale. Permission for this scheme was refused by the then Minister of Housing and Local Government and Longsleddale survived yet another threat.

54

The mile-long avenue of ancient oaks in Levens Park, near Kendal. A public footpath runs through the avenue. In 1968 when the route of the M6 – Kendal link, designed as dual 24ft carriageways, was under discussion, a line was chosen by the Ministry of Transport which cut through the northern end of Levens Park and the oak avenue. Only after prolonged representations at the highest level was the Minister of Transport, who eventually came to see the site himself, persuaded to hold a public inquiry.

In October 1970, at the opening ceremony of the M6 through Westmorland, the Minister of Transport announced that he had decided that the route of the Kendal link road should be outside Levens Park.

Ambleside. The question of a bypass for Ambleside has been under discussion since the 1930s and has taken a number of forms. The highway authority's 1970 scheme was grandiose. It commenced the reconstruction half a mile south of Waterhead and included lengths of dual carriageway with large roundabouts, junctions, embankments and modern concrete bridges. This scheme visualized the road running through the parkland and meadows to the west of Ambleside – beautiful countryside in the valley of the River Rothay enjoyed by residents and visitors for its tranquillity and mountain views. Millans Park, with its paths, its tumbling becks, and stone footbridge was a safe playground for children as well as the way to the fells for thousands of holiday-makers. The loss of this area to a vast new highway of a design completely alien to the heart of the Lake District seemed intolerable. In the face of widespread objections, modified schemes were prepared which reduced the scale of both the road and the engineering structures and took a line close under Loughrigg Fell. However, after a public inquiry the Secretary of State decided that a one-way system should first be tried for Ambleside.

Staveley from Reston Scar looking eastwards towards Kendal. Staveley is just within the National Park boundary and lies astride the A591, the Kendal–Windermere–Ambleside–Keswick road. This is the principal route from the South into the Lake District. Leaving the M6 motorway at the Farleton interchange (no. 36) there is a dual-carriageway road to the National Park boundary at the northern end of the Kendal bypass some two miles before Staveley is reached. In 1973 Westmorland County Council applied for planning consent for the construction of a dual 24ft carriageway road to bypass the village of Staveley on the southern side, that is, through the fields on the right-hand side of the illustration. The Planning Board refused the application on the grounds that the construction of a high-speed dual-carriageway road would be out of character with the Lake District National Park and contrary to the Board's policy of maintaining the A591 as a predominantly single-carriageway road. A public inquiry into the issue was held in January 1974, when the County Council contended that there should eventually be a dual-carriageway road as far as Cook's House Corner at Windermere with the Staveley bypass designed to fit into this policy. F.L.D. supported the Planning Board at the inquiry, agreeing that while Staveley should be bypassed the scale of the road planned was too great. The Inquiry Inspector in his report said that in his view a dual-carriageway road should not be taken so far inside the National Park as Windermere. He felt that a greater enjoyment of the Park by the public would flow from a slower approach to the central area. Further he saw that a dual-carriageway road attractive to through industrial traffic would make it more difficult to control the use of the A591 as was planned. The Minister agreed with the Inspector and the appeal by the County Council was dismissed. Plans for a single-carriageway bypass are now being prepared.

57

Great Gable from Innominate Tarn, Haystacks, scenery with mountain, crag, and tarn, typical of the dramatic centre of the Lake District. It was wild country such as this, where there is little evidence of the hand of man, that inspired the early campaigns for its designation as a National Park. F.L.D.'s first statement of policy, urging that the Lake District be made a National Park, was issued in June 1937. It pushed continually for the establishment of a strong National Parks Commission to give support and guidance, and to bring a unified policy for administering the Lake District, then divided among the Counties of Cumberland, Westmorland, and Lancashire. Under the Planning Act of 1947 each County planned its own piece of the Lake District. It was wrong, F.L.D. said, that the same planning machinery should apply to the Lake District, a proposed National Park area, as applied to Leicestershire or Rutland. By April 1948 the Minister of Town and Country Planning was, in the opinion of F.L.D., still prevaricating; he had had 12 months to consider the Hobhouse Report yet his only comment was 'it must be adequately studied'. The Minister, it was feared, had rejected the main principle of the Hobhouse Report, that there should be a special National Park Planning Committee, fully executive in its own right, of which half the members would be representatives of the 'national' interest, nominated by a National Parks Commission, and the other half nominated by the County Councils. It was evident too that the National Parks Commission was to be merely an advisory body.

In 1947 F.L.D. foresaw a long struggle with continued conflicts if the Lake District was to be protected from diverse threats. In the then absence of National Parks legislation and of effective planning of the Lake District as an undivided whole, it was upon organized voluntary effort (as in the Peak District, which in all essentials had the same problems) that the main duty of watchfulness rested and the main burden of opposing all wrong-headed schemes.

Services. Claims for their release were the subject of dispute on which the Government said no decision could be taken until 1952. The Society also feared that at any time there would be a new crop of 'regional' water schemes with new dams, flooded valleys, and their 'varied by-products'. They could see a hydro-electric monster, lurking, round the corner.

In the autumn of 1947 Barrow Corporation, which then ran the electricity undertaking for that area, had surveyed Eskdale and the Duddon Valley for a hydro-electricity scheme which required two reservoirs in Upper Eskdale, four generating stations in the Duddon Valley, and two reservoirs there, one above Seathwaite and the other nearer to the village. F.L.D. was anticipating that the proposal would engender a country-wide campaign of opposition. As it was, with the nationalization of the electricity industry, the scheme never progressed beyond the drawing boards. In those post-war days it also seemed to F.L.D. that the threat of afforestation, particularly of common land, successfully fought off in the 1930s, was again gaining strength.

The Society's main drive however was for the designation of the Lake District as a National Park, and for continual scrutiny of the legislation and its application. At this time F.L.D. appointed a full-time Secretary, Philip Cleave, and set up an office in Ulverston. The Society's income in 1948 was less than £1,500 a year and total assets amounted to £3,250. By 1978 income had grown to £15,000 a year and total assets to over £45,000.

58

Upper Eskdale and the eastern precipices of Scafell, an area threatened in the mid forties by a hydro-electric scheme. In 1948, a year before the passing of the National Parks Act, F.L.D. saw the position of the Lake District as little short of desperate. In an appeal for funds and members the Society's leaflet said that there were still three major threats to the Lake District, naming first the training areas still held by the

59

The National Park in winter. Derwent Water looking across the frozen lake to Manesty Woods and Maiden Moor.

The Tourist Board has attempted over the years to lengthen the visiting season and to stimulate interest in the Lake District in winter. These efforts have scarcely been successful. It remains difficult to find hotel accommodation in the months from mid November to mid February because there is little

demand. The Lake District is alpine and spectacular on a winter's day of snow and frost and blue sky, but such conditions are infrequent and exceptional in most winters and cannot be forecasted. There have only been two or three occasions in the past 20 years when skating has been possible on Derwent Water. A snow fall, or a wind when the lake is freezing, will so roughen the ice, as in the illustration, to make skating difficult or impossible. Skating at Tarn Hows or at Ratherheath, near Kendal, takes place a little more often but is equally unpredictable.

60

Great Langdale from above Harry Place, with Bow Fell, snow-streaked, in the background. The Pikes in the middle distance, with their prominent and familiar outline, are common land. The Lake District is rich in common land which includes large areas of its mountainous centre. There has always been a high degree of access on foot on the Lake District mountains, although there is not always a legal right to this. The Langdale Pikes, Grasmere, and other commons which were in the former Lakes Urban District are among those to which, however, there *is* a legal right to walk anywhere under the provisions of Section 23 of the Law of Property Act 1925. This Section made commons in Urban Districts subject to free and open access. It was a strange circumstance, and in this case a happy one, which made the centre of the Lake District an Urban District.

F.L.D. has from its inception been concerned with the protection of common land and the preservation of rights upon it. The Society carried out a survey of common land in the 1940s involving much field work, and compiled maps and other information which became invaluable in later years. In 1956 the Society submitted lengthy and detailed evidence in writing to the Royal Commission on Common Land. (F.L.D. *News-Letter*, June 1957.) The Commission recommended the compilation of a register of commons and commoners' rights, and this became the subject of legislation in the Commons Registration Act 1965. In the late 1960s when the registers were being built up, F.L.D. registered many commons and village greens. Some have been the subject of objections which remain unresolved and will in due course come before a Commons Commissioner for decision.

61

Walking party having lunch in March sunshine at Stickle Tarn, Great Langdale. Snow drifts pattern the slopes of Harrison's Stickle and the tarn is still frozen. It is the Lake District being enjoyed as the early promoters of National Parks and the legislators visualized it should be. Such terrain as this appears to be in little danger of change or development, but it can suffer from over-use. The track to Stickle Tarn from the large National Trust car park and from the New Dungheon Ghyll Hotel is one of the most worn and wide in the Lake District. There is also the question of larger numbers of people in the mountains detracting from an essential quality of wild country – its loneliness and solitude. Stickle Tarn in its great rocky amphitheatre is a dramatic place, to be reached by some effort, and to be appreciated only in quietude. On most occasions it is found so, apart from the hours around noon on sunny summer days, and for shorter periods on good winter days.

The Sandford Committee (1974) made important pronouncements on recreation in National Parks, recommending the following broad categories:

a. areas of special importance for nature conservation, which are highly sensitive to pressure, access to which should be discouraged

b. areas of wild and relatively remote country which is of scenic and wild-life value, where access on foot, cycle, or horseback is appropriate, but where penetration by motor vehicle should be limited

c. areas of good farmland and productive woodland, access to which will be limited to rights of way or other defined routes and where facilities for visitors would be self-contained, for example an enclosed picnic site

d. areas suitable for intensive recreational use which should be developed to absorb visitors, and where large-scale facilities such as the major car parks and information centres should be concentrated.

The Sandford Report went on to say that the recreational uses of National Parks must be compatible with the qualities of the parks among which a sense of tranquillity and of contact with nature seemed to the Committee to be of especial value. Provision should not be made in National Parks for noisy pursuits be they on land or water or in the air.

62

Scafell's north-western precipices, mountaineering and rock-climbing terrain at the heart of the Lake District, open to all who have the energy to climb the slopes and the skill to scale the crags. Scafell is the second highest mountain in England (3,162ft) and may be ascended from Wasdale or Eskdale and other dale-heads in three or four hours without rock-climbing, although the routes are steep, rough, and stony. Section 5 of the National Parks Act 1949 says:

1. The provisions of this part of the Act shall have effect for the purpose of preserving and enhancing the natural beauty of the areas specified in the next following subsection, and for the purpose of promoting their enjoyment by the public.

2. The said areas are those extensive tracts of country in England and Wales as to which it appears to the National Parks Commission that by reason of (a) their natural beauty, and (b) the opportunities they afford for open-air recreation, having regard to both their character and to their position in relation to centres of population, it is especially desirable that the necessary measures shall be taken for the purposes mentioned in the last foregoing subsection.

The Act does not refer to 'relatively wild country' but to areas affording opportunities for open-air recreation, which apparently meant extensive areas of unenclosed fell and moorland where people could roam without restriction. In the 1940s, although National Parks were envisaged for all who wished to enjoy them, including motorists, they were thought of as basically for walkers, cyclists, campers, and naturalists. The Minister of Town and Country Planning referred in Parliament to the legislation as 'a people's charter for the open air, for hikers and ramblers, for everyone who loves to get out into the open air and to enjoy the countryside'.

63

Footpath near Patterdale with gate provided by the Upland Management Service. Stage one of what in its beginning was called the Upland Management Experiment started in 1969. It covered a relatively small part of the Lake District, the Patterdale, Hartsop, and Martindale areas. The purpose was to carry out small jobs to enhance the appearance of the countryside and provide for visitors' enjoyment of it. It also aimed to help farmers by reducing the conflict caused by visitors, by such work as repairing damaged walls or way-marking footpaths through valley-bottom land. The Experiment was to study how farmers might be encouraged to partake more positively in landscape conservation and recreation. The work was funded by the Countryside Commission. The practical aspects of the scheme were generally recognized by both the farming and the amenity and recreational interests as being well worth while and successfully carried out. A second stage of the Experiment started in 1973 and extended the area to include Ambleside, Grasmere, Rydal, Langdale, and Borrowdale, in short to cover about a third of the National Park. At this stage a full-time project officer was employed. The Countryside Commission bore 75 per cent of the expenditure and the Planning Board the remainder. Out of these experiments there has grown the Upland Management Service with extended functions in the sphere of tourism and landscape management. The service now covers the whole of the National Park.

Eroded footpath on The Band, the popular route from Great Langdale to Bow Fell and Crinkle Crags. There are a number of paths in the Lake District which have reached this kind of condition. The extent of the damage naturally depends on the scale of use, the nature of the surface, and steepness. Once the surface layer is broken or the vegetation is worn away, water, particularly in heavy storms, is the destructive agent. There has been a great deal of study of this problem but no ready solution has been found. Drainage work has been undertaken, and diversions and new less susceptible routes have been introduced, in some places with considerable success. It would be wrong to reconstruct paths in an over-formalized or obtrusive manner or carry out work which would be difficult to maintain. It would be wrong to limit the sense of freedom in the hills by too much guidance or by restrictions on the variety of routes which could be taken. Some methods of dealing with erosion can be worse and more damaging than the worn path itself, such as untidy posts and rope or wire directing progress in wild places, or the use of nylon matting and netting on mountain slopes, as in some parts of Scotland. Some of the badly eroded paths, such as those from Striding and Swirrel Edges to the summit of Helvellyn, pose the question of the acceptability of artificial works in wild and remote places as well as raising enormous practical problems. The Planning Board's aim in the National Park is to ensure that the character of the fells is protected by avoiding unnecessary path improvements whilst at the same time remedying the worst effects of over-use.

65

A walker at the ancient British hill-fort on Castle Crag, Shoulthwaite. The path, a right of way to this interesting site, begins about 100yd north of the Thirlmere dam; it passes between stone gateposts into the forest and then climbs steeply among the trees. The Manchester Water Act 1879 which authorized the construction of the reservoir provided that 'the access heretofore actually enjoyed on the part of the public and tourists to the mountains and fells surrounding Lake Thirlmere . . . shall not be in any manner restricted'.

Under Part IV of the National Parks Act 1949, a duty was placed on highway authorities to survey and map every public right of way. F.L.D. decided that it was necessary to check the draft maps which were produced by the highway authorities, then the three County Councils of Cumberland, Westmorland, and Lancashire, as far as the Lake District and its environs were concerned. The checking of the paths for

accuracy of the routes shown, the endeavour to ensure that there were no omissions, and the preparation of material for the authorities, involved a great deal of voluntary work on the part of F.L.D. In both Westmorland and Lancashire it proved possible to make informal arrangements with the County Councils for a large number of omitted paths to be added to the draft maps in their pre-publication stage, by agreement with Parish or District Councils. In Cumberland the late Revd. H. H. Symonds, then F.L.D. Chairman, attended a number of hearings, and as a result a considerable number of omitted paths were recovered. In many other cases the paths claimed were not agreed upon and representations had to be put at formal public hearings. This went on throughout the 1950s. F.L.D. believed that access on foot enabled the Lake District to be enjoyed in the most satisfying way, and the Society contributed much in effort and finance to this end.

Brothers Water, Patterdale, looking into the deep narrow valley of Dovedale. Hartsop Hall is across the lake among the trees. The conical peak on the left is High Hartsop Dod; Lowwood on the right. On 27 March, 1974, the Secretary of State confirmed by-laws made by the Lake District Planning Board for the control of boats on 20 of the small lakes and tarns. Brothers' Water is one of these. The by-laws were the first to be made by a National Park Authority under the powers given by Section 13 of the Countryside Act 1968. This is a very valuable Section, the inclusion of which was only obtained at the eleventh hour as a result of strong representations by the Planning Board and the amenity organizations. The by-laws prohibit the use on specified lakes and tarns of any vessel propelled by an internal combustion engine, with certain exceptions for rescue and safety operations and police and local-authority use. The powers of Section 13 came just in time to control the use of lakes and tarns; had they not existed or had the National Park Authority not taken advantage of them, it is certain that, with the increasing use of light transportable craft and outboard engines, these lakes and tarns would by now have lost a large measure of their peace and tranquillity.

Fishermen on the old 'Kirby Quay', near the head of Coniston Water. This quay was formerly used for loading slate from the quarry above the village for transport to Nibthwaite quay at the southern end of the lake. Coniston Water, popular with fishermen, contains trout, pike, perch, and, for the discerning, char. The use of the lake for power-boating has been resented not only by anglers, but by yachtsmen, canoeists, rowers, and other quiet and peaceful users of the lake. In the late 1950s a Mr Thomas Blackburn, being concerned about the future use and development of Coniston Water, purchased the bed of the lake which had been divided into three separate sections, each separately owned. The lake bed was then conveyed to trustees, known as the Rawdon-Smith Trust, which is administered by Coniston Parish Council. Clause 3 of the Trust Deed expressed the purpose of the Trust to be 'to preserve the Trust property in perpetuity under local control for the purpose of affording to the public facilities for recreation'. In January 1962 there was an appeal against the refusal of planning permission for the use of land and buildings at Ruskin Pier for the hiring of motor boats. The appeal was dismissed. The Inspector said, 'There is however also a need for some lakes to be reserved for those who value solitude, quietness, and a study of nature in unspoilt surroundings and Coniston Water can still in the main provide such conditions'. There had however been a growing use of the lake by water-skiers and for power-boating, leading to unpleasant confrontations and dangerous incidents. The summer of 1978, with the new by-laws in operation, showed a marked change to quieter and pleasanter conditions.

Limefitt Camp and Caravan Site in the Troutbeck
Valley above Windermere. The site was for many
years the subject of discussion and comment. It grew
from modest beginnings in the fifties when the farmer
permitted camping in his fields. The farm changed
hands and its commercial development for tourism
began on a much larger scale with various activities
which upset the local residents and other people. For
instance, at one period early on Sunday mornings the
camp tannoy played hymns which echoed distortedly
throughout the valley, an ironical choice being 'All
Things Bright and Beautiful'. The camp management
ceased this practice when they were told, to their
evident surprise; that the music was not appreciated
by the dale's inhabitants. Certain planning
permissions for the site were given for a limited period
only, against which condition the owner appealed. At

a public inquiry in March 1973 a great deal of
opposition to the site was expressed, especially to its
size and its lack of screening. The Inspector in his
report recognized that there were 'contrived facilities
provided at Limefitt, particularly those more
sophisticated and normally associated with holiday
camps, which tend to result in the destruction of the
very surroundings which are its primary attraction. . .
Since this is a contentious site and because of the great
potential for irreparable damage to this part of the
national heritage, special scrutiny is necessary in these
particular surroundings.' The Inspector recommended
that the appeal should be dismissed and that the
planning permission should remain temporary. The
Secretary of State did not accept this recommendation
and allowed the appeal. The site is now therefore a
permanent one.

69

An Easter Caravan Club Rally at Grasmere. Caravan clubs enjoy certain exemptions from planning control. No application for a site licence or planning permission is required from recreational organizations that have been recognized by the Secretary of State, for use by their members of land for camping or caravanning. The Caravan Club is such an organization and has been responsible for issuing almost all site certificates in the National Park. The Club consults the Planning Board before certifying a site and the Board's views are usually adequately taken into account. Exempted organizations may also hold caravan rallies. The Board and the amenity organizations have been critical in particular of this activity. Over recent years rallies have increased in number and size, sometimes congregating several hundred vans. The rallies at Grasmere and on the shores of Ullswater are of this size, they are in

particularly exposed places, and are within an area of special control. Rallies encourage more caravans into the National Park and where the same fields are repeatedly used by a series of organizations they become in effect permanent sites. In the National Park Plan the Board expressed the view that it was necessary to curb the privileges of exempted organizations as regards locations, size, and the frequency of rallies.

Caravans also have some exemption from strict planning control under what is known as 'the 28 day rule', a provision of the Town & Country Planning General Development Order 1977, S.I. 289. This permits any landowner to station, on a holding of not less than five acres, not more than three touring caravans for up to 28 days in any twelve-month period.

70

A screened secluded caravan site on the southern boundary of the Lake District. The control of caravans, both static and touring, has been a subject on which strong and divergent opinions have been held. There is now planning consent for over 7,000 holiday caravan pitches in the National Park, of which about 1,500 are allocated to touring caravans. The number of caravan pitches has increased more than ten-fold in the past 25 years and can now accommodate more people than all the Lake District hotels, guest houses, and other serviced accommodation. It is generally accepted that too many caravans can be greatly detrimental to the appearance and character of the Park. The Planning Board, in the Development Plan Review 1965, defined areas in which it considered caravans to be unacceptable and these covered largely the central and narrower dales and the lake shores. The National Park Plan 1978, defined four additional areas where beauty, quietude, and accessibility made them particularly susceptible to caravans and to which it was held that special control should apply; these are the Derwent Valley (below Bassenthwaite Lake), the Vale of Lorton, the Lowther Valley, and the Winster Valley. Even on the fringe of the Park there are few areas where new sites could be located, and these areas in any case are often important from the point of view of nature conservation even if they are scenically less dramatic. The National Park Plan indicated that it was very unlikely that any further pitches would be allowed for static vans. In 1973 the Board commenced a policy of requiring caravans on static sites to be painted in specified camouflage colours, and this condition has been applied when permissions have come up for renewal. Eleven colours in the ranges of dark brown, grey and green are specified and there is no doubt that their use has done much to render caravans less conspicuous.

Car park at Finsthwaite provided by the Lake District Special Planning Board for its access land at High Dam. Provision for car parking in woodland has been an approved policy over the past decade and has the obvious advantage of reducing the impact of numbers of parked cars on the natural scene. It has however the disadvantage that it can destroy valuable woodland. The construction of the large car park in Great Wood, Borrowdale, has been criticized for this reason. But the motor car has to be put somewhere if the visitor is to be able to obtain proper enjoyment of the National Park away from his vehicle. The better solution is to select suitable sites for car parking and to screen them with trees. The car parks at Aira Green and at Glencoyne Bay on Ullswater are good examples of this policy. Trees were planted by the National Trust some years in advance of the making of the car park at the New Dungheon Ghyll in Langdale. The National Trust has also constructed a well-integrated car park at Quay Foot in Borrowdale where plentiful provision (for most times) is made among the old quarries and their tips, and where self-sown silver birches randomly grow. Roadside parking is often difficult in the Lake District where wall, hedge, or fence come close to a tarmac carriageway. Some paths, such as the south-west Windermere shore path, cannot be reached without walking some miles of narrow, and in summer heavily trafficked road, because of the lack of parking places at the beginning of the footpaths. In these situations small informal lay-bys should be provided.

The unacceptable face of tourism. A German mobile hotel by Ullswater at Glencoyne Bay. The coach draws a large trailer of furniture-van proportions which accommodates the sleeping bunks in separate cupboard-like compartments, each with a window, as seen on the near side. The rear part of this vehicle is fitted out as a kitchen and the party is thus self-contained. In fine weather tables and chairs are set out café-fashion around the kitchen door. The mobile hotel requires a great deal of road space, large car parks, and large turning areas. On the narrow roads of the Lake District it is certainly out of place and causes inconvenience to other tourists. The journeys have of course to be limited to those places where there is room to manoeuvre and space to park to prepare meals and find other necessities. The mobile hotels of this type travel widely, going among other places to North Africa where presumably there is more room than in the Lake District.

The illustration also shows the shore in Glencoyne Bay, formerly much used for parking cars. In 1974 the National Trust provided a parking area across the road, having some years previously planted, in anticipation, a tree screen on the west side. Vehicles are now prevented by posts and boulders from driving on to the beach; this area is left open for picnicking, fishing, swimming, and boating.

73

Camp site near Brothers Water; Dovedale in the background. The illustration was taken from the Kirkstone Pass road (A592). In 1970 the Lake District Planning Board made an order (Town & Country Planning Act 1962, Section 28) requiring the discontinuation of the use of this site for camping and caravanning. The Board contended that, because it was so exposed, the site was scenically damaging in an area of high landscape value. There was an appeal against the Order, followed by an inquiry. The Inspector in his report said, 'That bearing in mind his findings of fact he was of the opinion the camp should be retained because it helped to meet the need, otherwise inadequately provided for, to accommodate people wishing to walk and climb in the dales and on the greater mountain masses in this area. Its position near the main road and the Brotherswater Hotel at the foot of Dovedale, and between two extensive mountain areas, was convenient for this purpose. Because the surroundings were beautiful and unspoilt and because the site could be seen to a limited extent from the road and from the mountains, it was desirable that the use should be confined to tents, which was more acceptable than caravans in this environment. The number of tents should be limited so that the character and appearance of this camp might be retained as a facility mainly for walkers and climbers rather than as an ordinary holiday-makers' camp'. In his view, 'Eighty tents could be accommodated mainly around the edge of the field without being too obtrusive. The period of use should be limited in order that the turf might recover and be preserved by grazing so that there should be a long period of the year when this place could be seen as a spot where there was no modern development except for the road. Some tree-planting, though it would not screen the camp from view from the mountains, would soften its impact on the scene'. The Secretary of State accepted these findings and confirmed an amended order. The tree-planting, somewhat regimented, can be seen in this view.

74

A walking party near the summit of Scafell, enjoying physical recreation in 'wild and unspoilt countryside and peace and quiet'.

A women's outing arrives at Bowness-on-Windermere to enjoy fresh air, the scenery, and a trip down the lake on the steamer.

It is a statutory duty to promote the enjoyment by the public of the National Park, but the ways and the extent to which this should be done have been, over the years, matters subject to widely differing opinions. Tourism has become an important contributor to the economic welfare of the Lake District, but it has been contended that there must at some time be control over the influx of visitors if the beauty and the grandeur of the Lake District and the pleasure of the visitors themselves are not to be ruined. In recent years F.L.D. has criticized the activities and large expenditure of the Cumbria Tourist Board, the prime purpose of which is to market or 'sell' the area. This has sometimes been done in the worst possible taste,

for example one advertisement urged visitors to 'mountaineer by motor car' over the Hardknott and Wrynose passes, roads already crowded and dangerous enough without this encouragement. It has been claimed by F.L.D. and many others that the Lake District should be enjoyed as an area of beautiful countryside suitable above all else for walking and quiet recreation, and that there must be opposition to the provision of facilities which are unrelated to the concept of a National Park. In 1969 there was an application to establish an 'amusement arcade' at Bowness. This was refused by the Planning Board whose decision was upheld by the Secretary of State on appeal. F.L.D. submitted that development of this type was completely alien in the Park, and fortunately the Lake District remains without an 'amusement arcade' anywhere within its boundaries.

76

Ullswater from the sailing school at Glenridding. Ullswater has long been used for power-boating and water-skiing with, especially in recent years, increasing conflict with other interests, sailing, fishing, rowing, and in particular the quiet enjoyment of the shore, its paths, and the lower slopes of the mountains. Ullswater, like Windermere, Derwent Water, and Coniston Water, is governed by the by-laws made in the late 1950s under Section 249 of the Local Government Act 1933 with the intention of reducing noise from boat engines. No one, whether potentially prosecutor or prosecuted, seems to have taken any notice of them. On 1 January 1967 the Lake Ullswater (Collision Rules) Order was made. These rules are similar to those that apply to Windermere and deal with the display of lights, dangerous navigation, sailing rules; make special provisions concerning water-skiers; and define certain areas

where the speed limit should be 10 m.p.h. These areas in the case of Ullswater were comparatively small. At the 1977 inquiry into the by-laws to extend the 10 m.p.h. speed limit over the whole of the surface of the lake, much was made of the noise of power-boating; its dangers and unpleasantness to others, the vast majority of lake users; and to the irresponsible behaviour of 'cowboys' – water skiers and power-boaters who were not members of a Club and not subject to the disciplines of Club membership. The Ullswater by-laws were not confirmed but it was indicated that speed restrictions on the whole lake would be applied in five years' time without another inquiry. The opinion of the Inspector, that the water-skiers should have time to find or be provided with facilities outside the Lake District National Park, was accepted by the Home Secretary.

Coniston Water with the Old Man in the background on the left and Swirl How in the distance. Coniston village is amongst the trees to the right. The lake, five and a half miles long and only 870 yd at its widest, is beautifully set between the rolling moorland and mountains on the west and the forest and woodland on the east. Its western shores have remained almost unspoilt except for heavy use in summertime for camping and caravanning about Coniston Old Hall. Since the National Trust's purchase of this property and the farmland immediately to the south in 1971, the caravans have been moved away from the lakeside field into the adjoining Park Coppice. Other measures have been taken, such as providing alternative camping sites, and planting trees to reduce the impact

on the lake scene. There is a flourishing yacht club and the use of the lake for sailing is extensive. Public access to the eastern shore is almost continuous, with a minor and attractive road running close to the water. The Forestry Commission and the National Trust have provided a number of parking places, some with picnic tables, in the woodland, and these are well sited and well used. Simple boating in rubber dinghies, canoes, and in small sailing craft is popular from this eastern shore, particularly from the shingly spit south of Brantwood and the shores of Park-a-Moor. The National Trust and other owners have prohibited the launching of powered craft from their shorelines around the lake but a greater degree of control over this practice was achieved when the by-laws which limit the speed of powered craft to 10 m.p.h. over the whole lake came into operation in 1978.

78

Derwent Water and Skiddaw. Derwent Water is a small lake, not three miles long and less than a mile across, surrounded by natural woodlands and shapely and dramatic mountains. There is a high degree of freedom to enjoy the lake surface, to land upon its islands (with the exception of Derwent Isle) and to walk about its shores, which are largely owned by the National Trust. At the public inquiry of 1976 on the power-boat by-laws it was contended by the National Trust, F.L.D., and others that the by-laws did not go far enough in the case of Derwent Water, and that it was not a question of controlling speed on this lake but prohibiting power-boating, with the exception of the service provided by the public launches. In fact three years earlier the Planning Committee of the Lake District Planning Board had recommended a by-law for this stricter purpose, but unfortunately the Board rejected this by as close a vote as 11 to 10.

Marina near Ferry Nab on Windermere. Windermere is the most heavily used of all the lakes in the Lake District National Park. There are about 1,000 moorings on and around the lake. Collision Rules made under the Merchant Shipping Act 1894 have applied to the lake in one form or another for more than 70 years. The current rules are set out in the Lake Windermere (Collision Rules) Order 1973. They cover navigation requirements, lay down speed-limit zones, and impose particular conduct on water skiers. It was contended by a number of witnesses at the Three Lakes Inquiry that banning water-skiing from Ullswater and Coniston Water would bring increased pressure on Windermere. This Inquiry, in 1976, considered

Planning Board by-laws to limit the speed of powered craft to 10 m.p.h. on Ullswater, Coniston Water, and Derwent Water, a restriction that would also prevent water-skiing. The considerable number of people who used the first two lakes would, it was thought, go to Windermere for their sport. The Inspector reported however, that in his opinion the problem of Windermere should be dealt with by a more rigid enforcement of the existing Collision Rules aided by a system of regulation directed towards a better identification of offenders. The Lake District Special Planning Board has now made by-laws requiring the registration of all powered craft used on Windermere.

80

Hawkshead in 1973. Hawkshead is a unique village with its white buildings clustering, unplanned, about the small square and narrow streets leading to it, which are overhung by the upper storeys of the houses. Alleyways run between the buildings and beyond footpaths begin; to the east across the meadows to Claife Heights and to the west over the undulating country to Tarn Hows. Many of the buildings date from the 17th and 18th centuries. The village was built for people on foot or horseback; its scale is not small: it is minute. The F.L.D. Traffic Management Report said, 'To see a heavy lorry or large motor coach in Hawkshead is to experience incongruity at its limit'. There was therefore no objection in principle when in 1972 Lancashire County Highways Authority produced a scheme for a bypass, euphemistically called a 'relief road' to the east of, and close to, the village. It was part of the scheme, and one of which F.L.D. stressed the importance, that

upon the completion of the relief road the passage of traffic through the village should be prohibited. Paved areas were planned for the 'narrows' (being negotiated by the 'bus in the illustration) and for other points which would prevent through vehicular traffic, but entry was permitted from the north and south for deliveries and essential services. Consultations and discussions took place about the line and design of the bypass and this was opened for Spring Bank Holiday, 1974. F.L.D. complained that the restrictions put on traffic using the village streets were not effective enough as they relied only on notices which prohibited entry to the village, except for access. This type of control is extremely difficult to enforce as the definition of 'access' is so wide and vague. The original scheme of paving certain points was not carried out so that this unique and beautiful village has not reaped the full benefit of the bypass.

81

Dumped cars and litter off a minor road. In the early 1960s abandoned cars were a growing menace in the countryside. An attempt was made to deal with some of the more prominent examples in the Lake District by a voluntary working party composed of members of F.L.D. and National Park Voluntary Wardens; it came to be known as the 'heavy gang'. Cars were removed from such damaging situations as the shore of Blea Tarn, from fields in Great Langdale, from Subberthwaite Common and from roadside verges in Ennerdale, Eskdale, and Dunnerdale. It was hard work for which the volunteers had to provide their own equipment. The local authorities were sometimes unhelpful about the use of their tips for the disposal of wrecked cars and litter; the gates were locked at weekends when the work was usually done and it was difficult to make special arrangements. The Civic Amenities Act 1967 improved the situation. It placed upon local authorities a duty to provide tips for old and useless cars and it gave local authorities powers to move abandoned cars. It also required the provision of tips to which there is public access for the disposal of litter. The Planning Board in recent years has employed paid staff to collect litter. Regular visits are made to car parks, viewpoints, and lake shores. Roadside verges also receive attention. At the present time eight men and four vans are employed in summer time and two men and two vans operate throughout the year.

82

The ridge of Blencathra, looking westwards. Derwent Water can be seen in the valley to the left and the distant peak of Grisedale Pike is catching the sun. The A66, now a major highway, runs at the foot of the crags and slopes of Blencathra. The movement for National Parks and access to the countryside was led in the forties by C.P.R.E., strongly supported in the Lake District by F.L.D. and by the Ramblers' Association. The idea of establishing National Parks had first been examined by the Government in 1929 but the great step forward came with John Dower's Report to the Minister of Town and Country Planning in April 1945.

For some years John Dower was a member of the Executive Committee of F.L.D. and he was also involved in 1936 in drawing up the maps showing areas to be protected from afforestation.

83

The Lake District Ski Club Hut at 2,500 ft on Raise, Helvellyn. The north-facing slopes of this area, because they tend to retain snow drifts well into the spring, became the centre for the Ski Club's activities. The building and other works received planning permission and are the subject of licence between the Club and the National Trust. It is a condition of the permission that the hut should not be used for overnight accommodation. The Planning Board, which acquired Glenridding Common in 1977, owns the area in which the hut is situated jointly with the National Trust. The Board co-operates with the Club and the National Trust to maintain a high standard of management of the facilities on Raise and to ensure that the impact of the development on the surrounding areas is minimized. The Board has said that there must not be any large increase in the amount of snow-fencing, that there must be careful control over litter, and that the sensitive plant habitat must not be damaged. There are some species-rich flushes and mires close to the Ski Club's facilities.

Glenridding Common, the total extent of which is some 2,500 acres, is of particular botanical importance, there being rare alpine plants on the rock ledges along the extensive crags, and an area of juniper below Stang End. Some measure of protection is now given to these native communities by the Wild Creatures and Wild Plants Act 1975, which makes it an offence to uproot any wild plant, including lichen, and to pick, uproot, or destroy any plant specifically protected by the Act.

Flodder Allotment, the central and highest point of the limestone ridge of Whitbarrow. The cairn commemorates the work of Canon G. A. K. Hervey, who founded the Cumbria Naturalists' Trust. Whitbarrow is one of 24 reserves of the Cumbria Naturalists' Trust, eight of which are in the National Park.

The Lake District Special Planning Board has a statutory duty to conserve and enhance wildlife resources, to protect rare species and habitats, and to preserve sites of geological and physiographic importance. A number of other agencies are also concerned with nature conservation in the National Park. The Nature Conservancy Council is the official statutory body, working in co-operation with the Board and a number of voluntary organizations. These include, beside the Cumbria Naturalists' Trust, the Royal Society for the Protection of Birds, the county geological societies, and a number of local natural-history societies and field clubs. Nature conservation has attracted an increasing amount of attention in the last few decades, as indicated by the establishment and growth in membership of the voluntary societies. The Naturalists' Trust was established in 1962 as the Lake District Naturalists' Trust and in 1974 renamed the Cumbria Naturalists' Trust. In 1978 the membership was well over 2,000. Natural history societies in Cumbria have dramatically increased their membership. The National Park contains, because of its geological diversity and range of elevations, a multiplicity of wild-life habitats. There are four National Nature Reserves, namely Blelham Bog, North Fen Esthwaite, Roudsea Wood, and Rusland Moss. Extensive areas are designated 'Sites of Special Scientific Interest' and in total cover 13 per cent of the Park, including the Skiddaw massif, the Buttermere Fells, Martindale Forest, Helvellyn, and Fairfield.

Aira Force, Ullswater, a National Trust property. The National Trust has played a major role in protecting the natural beauty of the Lake District, preserving its traditional farming and providing access for public enjoyment. Its Lake District holdings are extensive and largely inalienable, covering in all about one-fifth of the area of the National Park. The first property acquired in the Lake District, in 1902, was Brandlehow Woods on the south eastern shore of Derwent Water. The Woods were bought by public subscription and handed over to the Trust for permanent preservation. All the early properties acquired were open spaces to which the Trust supporters wished the public to have continuing access. In 1906 Aira Force and Gowbarrow Fell were acquired and in 1908 Manesty, adjoining Brandlehow. Concern for the upper reaches of the dales dates from 1929 when the first farms were donated at the heads of Great Langdale and the Duddon Valley. The next 35 years saw the Trust's successful efforts to obtain control over other dale-heads, such as those of Wasdale, Borrowdale, and Eskdale. The Trust now owns 72 fell farms and several other lowland farms, together with the landlord's stock of sheep. All the Trust farms are let to tenants, and also 280 other cottages and houses, whenever possible to local people; only buildings unfit for permanent habitation are used as seasonal holiday accommodation. In 1961 the common land owned by Lord Lonsdale covering 17,000 acres and including the Langdale Pikes and Crinkle Crags was leased to the Trust. It also holds a large number of restrictive covenants over land and buildings which enable it to control any potential development or alterations. Despite this the Trust has seldom acted as a pressure group in Lake District affairs and policies when land or buildings not owned or protected by it have been at risk; this responsibility has been left to other bodies.

86

A National Park village, Askham, with its dwellings (many of them of the 17th and 18th centuries), set attractively about a spacious green. Conversions and modernizations have been carried out and new buildings constructed; but a close look about the village reveals incongruities. The main means of preservation has been by the Planning Board's powers of development control. The Dower Report said ' "Landscape preservation" is the generally accepted, although somewhat inadequate, description of the task of maintaining the characteristic landscape beauty of wide areas; inadequate because it suggests a purely negative process and an artificial and lifeless result. The most obvious and urgent requirements are, indeed, of a negative or restrictive nature. The first essential is to impose control over all kinds of building development or changes in the use of land; and to administer the control so as to prevent, except where they are shown to be essential in the national interest, all developments or changes, other than for agriculture, for open-air recreation and for a limited residential and tourist expansion of the existing centres – small towns and selected larger villages – in each National Park area. Where development of any kind is permitted, careful control must also be exercised over its form – siting, size, design, materials, and colours – so as to ensure that it harmonizes as fully as possible with its natural setting and with any neighbouring buildings'.

Windermere from the Claife shore near Harrowslack. The two islands named Lilies of the Valley in the middle distance. In the background lie the Troutbeck hills and the conical peaks of Froswick and Ill Bell. This is the ridge that divides Troutbeck from Kentmere. Belle Island, Windermere's largest island, is to the right and is privately owned, accommodating a handsome residence. Most of the other islands are owned by the Lake District Special Planning Board and landing on them is permitted. The Water Order that Manchester Corporation obtained in 1966 permitted abstraction from Windermere as well as from Ullswater. There had been opposition to this scheme also, but the use of Windermere did not raise the passionate feelings that were expressed about Ullswater. An underground pumping station was built at Calgarth, expensively excavated in solid rock and covered over, like the one at Parkfoot on Ullswater; both are only to be found by persistent searching. Cattle graze contentedly over the silent running machinery. Water drawn from Windermere is pumped to a covered balancing reservoir at Banner Rigg and then goes on to the treatment works at Watchgate north of Kendal. Other works authorized by the Order were the rebuilding of the weir at Newby Bridge and the raising of its height by six inches. Windermere does not seem to have suffered as a result of these waterworks, probably because the amount permitted (an average of 22 million gallons a day) is small in relation to the capacity of this great lake – it is over ten miles long – and its extensive catchment area.

Satterthwaite, a small hamlet in Grisedale. The pressure to convert barns, field houses, and other agricultural buildings into domestic accommodation and for holiday purposes has been felt throughout the Lake District over the past 25 years, and many prolonged and sometimes bitter arguments have ensued when planning permission has been refused. The Planning Board's refusal of permission to carry out conversions have frequently been upheld on appeal and this policy against the use of isolated barns for residential purposes has been confirmed by the Secretary of State. In 1977 the Board published a leaflet entitled *The Conversion of Barns*, setting out its general policy. The real need of an applicant is to be taken into account and if this cannot be shown it is unlikely that the conversion of a building would be allowed. The assessment is to be particularly rigid when the building is in an isolated position. Permission is more likely for conversions to buildings in towns or villages, subject to normal planning principles.

Various questions need to be asked about the impact of the proposed barn conversions on the countryside, taking into consideration the effects of new access roads, electricity supply lines, ancillary buildings, garages, extensive additions, and complete rebuildings. Where a farm building has been converted to provide tourist accommodation, the Planning Board endeavours to ensure that it remains part of the farm business and is not sold off, or developed independently of the farm. This has been done by means of planning conditions or the use of agreements made under Section 52 of the Town and Country Planning Act 1971, confining the accommodation to short-term letting.

Ennerdale: Anglers' Crag and Crag Fell from Bowness Point. The lake and a small part of the surrounding land is owned by the North West Water Authority but two-thirds of the shoreline and over 2,500 acres of land around it are owned by the National Trust. The crag and fell, as seen here on the far side of the lake, are part of the National Trust property. Ennerdale is as wild as any Lake District valley; no public road runs along its shores; it must be explored on foot. Access for the walker is good and virtually unlimited except for the physical restrictions of the denser afforestation. A right of way encircles the lake – the path close to the shore on the south side, running across Anglers' Crag and continuing to the lake head. This passes through natural woodland and is a particularly attractive stretch. At Bowness Point the public road ends, but there is encouragement to walk on by the forestry road along the lake shore or to explore the Commission's Smithy Beck Trail. On fine weekends this western end of Ennerdale is popular, but only the more energetic reach the secluded places in the valleys of Deep Gill and the Silver Cove Beck. The hardy and dedicated go on further up the dale to the wild rocky places such as Pillar Rock and Mirk Cove.

There are Youth Hostels, at Gillerthwaite two miles from Bowness Point, and at Black Sail a further four miles up the valley, for those who wish to explore Ennerdale thoroughly.

Thrang Quarry housing, Chapel Stile, Langdale. In 1966 application was made to the Lake District Planning Board for permission to build 26 holiday cottages on the site of the disused Thrang Quarry at Chapel Stile. The Planning Board refused permission on the grounds that sewerage facilities were inadequate. F.L.D. held the view that the development was inappropriate in this situation and that it would, on the edge of a small village and in the centre of Great Langdale, be damaging on both social and aesthetic grounds. It was contended that a small community could not be enlarged in this way without its character being changed, and that ribbon development of this design in particular would be very harmful to Langdale, one of the National Park's most

prized and visited parts. It was agreed that the then appearance of the quarry, from which many thousands of tons of spoil had been removed, was bad and required some treatment and consideration of its future use. This stretch of the valley had already been subjected to some urbanization by the construction of a new 30ft road with concrete kerbs. It was suggested to the Planning Board that the quarry site should be tidied, planted with trees, and provision made for car parking and picnic areas, facilities then much needed in this part of the valley. However, early in 1967 the housing scheme was resubmitted with the inclusion of a sewage disposal plant and was given planning approval, with the result to be seen today at Chapel Stile.

91

Terrace housing in Windermere, built in 1978. A
startlingly unattractive scheme in a Lake District town.

Tungsten mine in Mosedale, Mungrisdale, with the slopes of Carrock Fell on the left. Mosedale is a wild and unspoiled valley through which runs a narrow unfenced road alongside the River Caldew with its deep rocky pools and picnic places. The surroundings of Carrock Fell have been mined from the Middle Ages for various minerals, but the waste tips and abandoned buildings are now for the most part weathered and grown over. The present mine, for which planning permission was given in 1972, is situated close to the confluence of Grainsgill Beck and the River Caldew. This is now the only mine operating in the Lake District.

In 1971 there was a new mining threat to the Lake District. It was learnt that Manchester Corporation had given permission to Rio Tinto Finance and Exploration Limited to carry out tests on its Haweswater and Thirlmere estates for the purpose of discovering what minerals were there. The Company also sought

permission to make similar explorations from other landowners in the Lake District. This resulted in much public criticism. F.L.D. was completely opposed to new mining in the National Park and said that to permit prospecting was to 'invite the burglar into the house'. New mining would not be like the comparatively small operations of the past because the modern working methods of an organization such as Rio Tinto require vast amounts of earth-moving equipment, overhead ropeways, new access roads, heavy transport, and extensive tips. Such exploitation would cause havoc in the Lake District. Manchester Corporation withdrew its permission to prospect and as far as is known no commercial exploration has taken place in the Lake District, although tentative schemes are sometimes proposed for the treatment of tipped material. The policy of the Lake District Special Planning Board is that any new large-scale extraction will be opposed unless a compelling national need can be demonstrated.

93

Cattle wintering shed built in 1976 in the central Lake District. Its situation, design, and materials were subject to prolonged negotiations and the cost of its construction subject to considerable grant-aid. As a result there is no doubt that the building has materially less impact than the one originally proposed, which was to be of concrete and asbestos, prominently sited.

Under the Town and Country Planning General Development Order agricultural buildings were granted considerable exemptions from planning law. It has been contended frequently that it was anomalous and undesirable that certain forms of development which are of particular importance in National Parks, may be constructed without application for planning permission. A special notification procedure was introduced by the Town and Country Planning (Landscape Areas Special Development) Order 1950,

and applied to almost the whole of the Lake District National Park. The procedure enables the planning authority to require an application to be made if it considers the proposed design or materials to be unsatisfactory, but leaves the farmer free to proceed after 14 days if the planning authority takes no action.

The question of compensation and grants is an involved one. Compensation for extra costs to meet stringent design standards is not at present available where conditions relating to the design and external appearance are imposed under the Landscape Areas Order following receipt of a Notice of Intention. Compensation is payable where an appeal is made to the Secretary of State relating to the conditions imposed upon a planning consent, and the appeal is dismissed. This latter procedure applied in the case of the barn illustrated.

94

Winter grazing at Aira on the shores of Ullswater with St Sunday Crag in the background. The Hobhouse Committee (1947) accepted John Dower's definition of a national park but said 'Here are no vast expanses of virgin land . . . which can be set aside for public enjoyment or conservation of wild life. Instead we are dealing with a closely populated and highly developed country, where almost every acre of land is used in some degree for the economic needs of man and has its place in a complex design of agricultural, industrial, or residential use. Yet it is just because this is a densely populated and highly industrial country that

the need for National Parks is so pressing and that it is all the more urgent to ensure that some at least of the extensive areas of beautiful and wild country in England and Wales are specially protected as part of the national heritage'.

The Lake District was designated a National Park on 9 May 1951 and covers 866 sq. miles including the mountain massifs centred around Scafell, Skiddaw and Helvellyn, the towns of Keswick, Ambleside, and Windermere, the numerous lakes and tarns, and about 10 miles of coastline between Ravenglass and Silecroft.

Grasmere from the path to Alcock Tarn. This village in the heart of the National Park has been subjected to heavy pressures for development and by increased tourism. In 1977 the case of the Rothay Hotel illustrated some of these problems. (This gabled building can be seen in the illustration on the far side of the central field.) It was last used as an hotel in 1970 and has since that time stood empty and decaying. Various schemes for the use of the land and buildings were put forward. Two of these received planning permission, one for the conversion of the property to residential accommodation for retired teachers and another for use as holiday flats. Neither of these projects was pursued. Early in 1977 a development company sought permission to restore the hotel and convert it into five flats, with three ground-floor shops fronting on to the forecourt, and in addition the construction of 14 two and three-storey houses at the rear. Local opinion feared that such a large scheme in the centre of Grasmere would be highly detrimental to this small village and that the new building would stand out obtrusively among the scattered houses from many points on the amphitheatre of the surrounding fells. Grasmere remains largely unspoilt by new buildings of urban design and its unique situation in the mountainous centre of the Lake District is reason enough for giving it the highest degree of protection. The villagers, and many people from further afield, expressed these and similar views at a packed public meeting held in Grasmere. The Planning Board took into account these expressions of public opinion and refused the planning application. The people of Grasmere decided that the matter should not rest there and set up a Grasmere Village Society with the first object of acquiring the Rothay Hotel and about 10 acres adjoining the site, all owned by the building developers. The Grasmere Society was registered as a charity and on 28 June 1977 launched an appeal for £80,000. The property was acquired by the Village Society in 1978 with the intention of restoring it either as an hotel or for the housing of local people.

Herdwick flock on the slopes of Seat Sandal, Dunmail Raise. The farmer has brought the bale of hay from his Grasmere farm. Daily feeding is necessary in periods of snow cover for the sheep out on the common, which here runs over the mountain ridges and down to the enclosed land of Patterdale, Glenridding and Glencoyne. Until the mid 1970s the road over Dunmail Raise was unenclosed, but the large number of sheep slaughtered and injured by fast traffic made it necessary to fence both sides of the road. The fences were set back in the interest of amenity and a number of stiles provided for access. The approval of the Department of the Environment is required for the fencing of commons and in this case was granted without complications as there were no objections.

The Herdwick is a small coarse-woolled animal of great hardiness and agility. It has a strong homing instinct which usually keeps it to its own part, or heaf, of the open fell. Therefore farmers in the Lake District have from early times been able to manage flocks on unenclosed common grazings. Each farm has its own mark, a combination of a particular daub on the fleece with a distinctive nick on the ear. These markings are recorded in the local 'Shepherds' Guide' and serve to identify strays. Until recent times Herdwicks were not fed in winter but had to depend on what could be found on the hills. In hard winters they will eat anything green, including holly, ivy, and moss from rocks and walls. In spring short work is made of tree seedlings and herbaceous growth in general, with in consequence a degrading of the vegetation. Fortunately the wild daffodil is unpalatable.

Grazing on the summit of Stony Cove Pike with the Ill Bell ridge across the upper valley of Troutbeck. The grass (*Nardus stricta*) is pale coloured in the autumn sunlight. In the far distance, between the peaks of Froswick and Ill Bell, Ingleborough is seen. Dower said that the scenery of the National Parks owed the man-made element in its character above all else to farming – both the extensive grazing of the higher open land and the more or less intensive grazing, mowing, and cropping of the lower, fully enclosed land. Efficient farming must be recognized as a necessity both to the economy and appearance of the Lake District, and this has been repeatedly stated and woven into the policies of the planning authorities. Dower also held that in National Parks established farming use should be effectively sustained, indicating that agriculture should not give way to recreational use.

There is a great variety in the standards, methods, and efficiency of farming in the Lake District, and the years since the Dower Report have brought changes in outlook and circumstances. Between 1963 and 1975 there was a decrease of 26 per cent in the number of hill farms in the Lake District, due to amalgamations, and a decrease of 21 per cent in the numbers employed on the farms. Despite this, farming and related industries such as agricultural engineering and farm contracting are still important sources of employment. In 1971, 13.9 per cent of the total number of employed persons in the Lake District were in farming, compared with 6.8 per cent in Cumbria and 2 per cent in England and Wales.

Ennerdale Show held in fields near the shore of the lake at Bowness Point. This is one of the many Lake District shows to which the farmers bring their sheep, cattle, and dogs. There is horse riding and jumping, fell-running and 'Cumbrian' wrestling, competitions for cakes and wine-making and vegetable growing, hound trails, and various other amusements and stalls. They are annual occasions and meeting places for local people where business, pleasure, and politics are discussed.

In the campaigning days of 1945 and 1946, before the designation of the Lake District as a National Park, F.L.D. was saying in its leaflet 'Make the Lake District a National Park' that it would be one of the first duties of the local Planning and Management Committee 'to protect and to improve fell-farming as the main traditional employment and the foundation of the local economy and local life, to continue and encourage the traditional rural industries and to encourage the "tourist industry" as a needful part of the local economy.' Thirty years have not changed what was said, but there is now a statutory responsibility on the Planning Board to promote the social and economic well-being of the National Park.

The population of the National Park is about 40,000. It declined slightly between 1951 and 1971. The South Lakeland area of the Park is the most densely populated and the only one that has been increasing in numbers, the growth being mostly concentrated around the towns and commuter areas of Ambleside and Windermere. The rural areas have continued to decline. Allerdale (the north-west of the Park) as a District has declined slightly, but looking at its parishes a few, Loweswater, Embleton, and Keswick, have gained population. Copeland (the south-west) has declined, particularly between 1961 and 1971. Eden District (the north-east) lost population throughout the 1951 to 1971 period.

Between 1952 and 1976 about 5,000 new houses were constructed in the National Park although the population was decreasing. This apparent contradiction was explained in the National Park Plan by three factors; firstly the number of residents occupying any one dwelling had decreased sharply; secondly a large number of dwellings were second homes; thirdly more houses were let as holiday accommodation (the number in these last two categories was established as 1,758).

Greenside Mines, Glenridding. These lead mines, which were discovered in the middle of the 17th century, were worked until 1962. In 1959 the Atomic Energy Commission carried out a series of underground seismic test explosions here. The terraced tips are extensive and stretch away beyond the right of the illustration. It is plain that mining on this scale, which abandoned its workings in this state, ruined a once lovely valley and its mountain sides. Some ineffectual attempts were made to tidy up and screen the tips but there remains a scene of unsightly desolation. The grassing of the tips in the centre of the illustration did not disguise their nature and it seems that some reshaping should have been attempted.

Some buildings have been demolished and the mine entrances closed. Remaining buildings are being used as a Youth Hostel (not in the picture) and as bases for a variety of outdoor activities.

In 1977 the Lake District Special Planning Board acquired Glenridding Common with a major part of the remains of Greenside Mines and its workings, and has plans to improve the site. These mines, at 1,100 feet, have always provided a parking place sought by fell-walkers and, in the winter, snow-skiers, but the track from Glenridding is narrow and deeply pot-holed. The question of restrictions on its public use by cars is under discussion by the Planning Board.

100

The Hartsop Valley from Dubhow Crag. The hamlet of Hartsop lies in the valley to the left with Hartsop Dod rising beyond. The Kirkstone road is seen running across and then at the edge of the rectangular fields of the flat valley bottom, before it mounts the pass with Red Screes on the right. Further to the right the trees of Low Wood come down to the western shore of Brothers Water. This wood is an important example of hill oak, ash, and hazel woodland and is designated a Site of Special Scientific Interest by the Nature Conservancy Council.

The lake, and much of the land around it and beyond, including Low Wood, is owned by the National Trust. The Hartsop Valley was the subject of a detailed study in 1975 by Rural Planning Services for the Countryside Commission and the Lake District Special Planning Board: *A Study of the Hartsop Valley* (Countryside Commission). The Study analysed the nature of the landscape of the Hartsop Valley, and its management. It examined the current and likely future recreational use of the area and looked at this in the light of National Park objectives. An important part of the report was concerned with the farming of the area, its economy, and its effect on the landscape and recreation. This report, which contains a wealth of information about the Hartsop Valley, made a number of recommendations designed to integrate successful farming of the area with the basic National Park purposes, the conservation of the landscape, the enhancement of its natural beauty, and its recreational enjoyment.

101

Slate quarry at Elterwater. The Great Langdale road runs along the edge of the field in which the sheep are grazing. The building near the corner of the field is the Langdales Hotel. Concern about the effects of quarrying on the landscape of the Lake District goes back at least a century. In the 1880s there was vociferous objection to the opening of the slate quarries above Rydal on the grounds not only of the damage to the appearance of these slopes of Loughrigg but to interference to rights of way and danger to the public from falling rocks and boulders. An issue of the *Manchester Guardian* in 1889 reminded its readers that one of Wordsworth's favourite walks was across the footbridge at Rydal and on to the western shore of the lake above which quarrying was

then starting. 'If the cost of nationalising the Lake District be beyond the pockets of wealthy England, if manorial rights here cannot be bought out, surely we could demand a ministerial conservancy to interfere with property owners only when their acts were plainly antagonistic to the higher interests of the people? No mineral should be worked here without parliamentary consent. . . . The livelihood of lodging-house keepers depends on a Lake Country kept as unlike the rest of the world as it possibly can be, in the quiet enjoyment of its unimprovable beauty'.

Peak production of slate occurred between the 1870s and 1890s. In the last 35 years the number of slate quarries and the size of the work-force have steadily declined, leaving numerous abandoned workings.

Slate quarrying above the Honister Pass. At Honister quarrying has gone on since 1643 and working in recent years has been high up on the flanks of Fleetwith Pike. There has been recent application to the Lake District Special Planning Board to open up a new area above Warnscale Bottom and to tip waste into the cavities of abandoned workings. Permission was granted to do this.

The prominent situation of Bursting Stones Quarry on the southern face of Coniston Old Man has given frequent cause for complaint, in spite of the efforts by the planning authorities to control its impact by limiting the size of the entrance to the working face and of the tipping area.

In all quarrying operations the large percentage of waste is one of the main problems as it is virtually impossible to assimilate waste stone into the landscape. To remove it would be expensive and put an additional burden of heavy vehicles on steep narrow and twisting roads. But the provision of employment and the economic-value arguments do not disguise the fact that large lumps of the Lake District have been, and are being, removed and carted away or thrown down the mountain sides. A bond system would be one means of ensuring that finance was available for landscaping, restoration schemes, and the removal of buildings and plant at the expiry of planning permission or the cessation of operations. A more rigid control of quarrying in the National Park is necessary, and this should first be exercized in the review of existing operations. New quarrying should only be permitted if there is a proven national need.

103

Copper Mines Valley above Coniston. Coniston Old Man is on the left. The peak in the distance is Swirl How. The valley is scarred with tips, old workings, and the crumbling walls of buildings, here made less obtrusive by a shroud of snow. The building in the centre is the Youth Hostel and the one to the right is used by a climbing club; both were formerly used in connection with mining. Higher up and out of the picture on the slopes of the Old Man there has been extensive slate quarrying. The quarry, now working, Bursting Stones, is on the south-east face of the mountain and access is directly from Coniston by the Walna Scar track. The slate is processed at Moss Rigg near Tilberthwaite. In 1974 an application was made by the owners of Bursting Stones quarry to erect a 10,000 sq. ft processing building on the flattish area close behind the Copper Mines Youth Hostel. It was refused by the Lake District Planning Board and a public inquiry was held in October 1974. F.L.D. supported the Board. It was submitted that in spite of the past workings, the valley was a dramatic, imposing, and spectacular place through which many thousands of people passed on their way to the peaks and ridges of Coniston Fells. It was wrong to bring new industrial activity into this area with all the difficulties of providing access for heavy vehicles. The track from the valley was difficult and dangerous, running close to the deep gorge of Church Beck. The proposal of the quarry company to construct a new access route from Bursting Stones across the eastern face of the mountain to the Youth Hostel was a devastating one. The appeal was dismissed by the Secretary of State. So the valley remains a quiet and peaceful place, without industrial activity, serving the prime purpose of a National Park.

The Kirkstone Quarries as seen from the Pass. The road from Ambleside called 'The Struggle' runs across the foot of the picture. These workings are prominent in the landscape and have grown considerably over the last 10 years. New methods, mechanization, and the high proportion of waste have been responsible for the increased impact of this activity on the mountain scene. On the other hand it must be recognized that quarrying is a traditional Lake District industry and that there are difficulties in enforcing planning conditions imposed many years ago which may, in any case, now be inadequate to cope with different operating requirements. Kirkstone Quarry is an example of this. It was originally one of the many small disused slate quarries scattered about the Lake District which had largely merged into the landscape by weathering action and the passage of time. The quarry was reopened in a very small way early in 1950 when a local mason and stone carver made application to use the stone for his craft. It was proposed to concentrate on the large amount of rock on the quarry bed and working on the quarry face was expected to be almost insignificant, even over a number of years. The business expanded and an application to make extensions was made in 1963. Because of the difficulty of assessing the effects on the landscape made by this kind of continuing development the permission was limited to 15 years. However, this did not cover the full period of the applicant's lease and an appeal was lodged. Following a public inquiry the Minister extended the approval period to 25 years. This clearly illustrates that once a quarry has been firmly established with an expanding output, the planning authorities find it difficult to reverse or even slow down the process.

105

Limestone Pavement in the Orton area. Limestone encircles the central mountains of the Lake District and is particularly evident in the south and east of Cumbria. Within the National Park there are the ridges of Whitbarrow, Scout Scar, and Hampsfell at Grange-over-Sands, and to the east the upland areas of Shap, Orton, and Asby Fell. These all have large expanses of fissured, water-worn pavements and cliffs and scars which make up dramatic scenery. Some of the pavement areas have been exploited; the stones, water-worn into strange and fascinating shapes, have been removed for garden rockeries and other purposes. Over the last 20 years a number of Cumbrian pavements have been devastated. In some cases planning control has been at least partially effective, in others the process of enforcement has been slow and cumbersome. The destruction has gone on while the legal processes have been lengthily pursued.

Wastwater Screes. A steep craggy mountainside with great fans of scree plunging into the eastern shore of the lake, giving the scene a wild and primitive appearance. A National Trust path runs close to the shore and through the grounds of Wasdale Hall, giving extensive and dramatic views up the lake to the superb group of mountains at the dale-head dominated by Great Gable. This path leads to the outflow of the lake into the River Irt and on to Lund Bridge where it joins the path that runs from the foot of the screes along the left bank of the river. Here is the pump house, stone built and of barn-like appearance, from which the water flows to supply British Nuclear Fuels. During the war a ramshackle building was put up here for housing the plant to supply water to the Ordnance Factory at Drigg. In later years F.L.D. protested and the Ministry of Supply went to the considerable expense of surrounding the outer shell with stone and roofing it with slate; it also exercised some care in keeping the surrounding area uncluttered with ancillary works and stores. There were too, in 1958, a number of temporary hutments still standing at the foot of Great Hall Gill about a quarter of a mile below the pump house. F.L.D. obtained a pledge from the Ministry of Supply that these would be moved from this dramatic situation by the end of 1960. It was the Ministry's intention that the disintegrating buildings should be replaced by a dwelling for the pump-house attendant and they promised that this, as some compensation for its lonely and inappropriate situation, would be constructed in local style and materials. However, F.L.D. continued to press for the clearance of the old buildings from the site and by the time this was done it had been found possible to operate the pumps by remote control, obviating the necessity for an attendant and his dwelling. The solitude of the scene at the foot of Wastwater was in large measure restored.

Patterdale and the head of Ullswater. The A592 (Kirkstone to Pooley Bridge) road can be seen running from the left of the illustration, through the hamlet of Patterdale and on under the wooded slopes of Keldas by the shore of Ullswater to Glenridding. The Glenridding valley goes into the hills and Greenside Mine is visible at its junction with Swart Beck. The shingle beds at the delta of Glenridding Beck stretch out into the lake. In 1938 F.L.D., then a fairly new society, vigorously pursued the question of the silting and discolouration of Ullswater which was being caused by the effluent from the lead mine. F.L.D. members were urged to go to Ullswater to see the pollution themselves and to write to the press to say that in their opinion an 'obligation lies upon industrial capital employed in a district of special beauty to use special care so that the beauty is not damaged.' The mining company installed new settling tanks which proved little better. The matter dragged on until in 1942 resort had to be made to legal action. The National Trust, as a riparian owner of the lake, agreed to co-operate with F.L.D. which guaranteed a substantial sum towards technical and legal costs. The Trust issued a writ against the mining company but the Ministry of Supply, by virtue of the power conferred under the Defence Regulations, authorized the continuing operation of the mine on conditions which led to a considerable lessening of the nuisance. By 1944 F.L.D. reported that the volume of suspended matter brought down by the beck was on a small scale, and after that there seems to have been no more trouble.

Borrowdale from the path to King's How with Rosthwaite in the middle distance. A public electricity supply was taken into the valley in 1955 after many years of argument about undergrounding the cable, especially its cost. F.L.D. was hotly and repeatedly criticized for the stand it had taken before the war which had led, it was argued, to the withdrawal of the then private company's scheme and to the delay in the provision of a supply to Borrowdale. The Society had over the years held firmly to three principles; firstly, that electricity should be brought to Borrowdale; secondly, that in order to preserve the beauty of this most famous of all the valleys of England the supply line should be underground; and thirdly, that the entire cost should not be a charge on the consumers.

The scenery of Borrowdale has received the attention of many writers, poets, painters, and travellers, and many famous people have stood upon that most renowned of viewpoints, Friars Crag, to look across Derwent Water to the shapely mountains that enfold the lake. Beyond the hamlet of Grange, the dale narrows between steep, rocky, tree-clad slopes which early visitors found frightening. Castle Crag, itself clothed in trees, a huge pinnacle of rock, stands in these narrows which are called the Jaws of Borrowdale. The twisting valley road goes on by disused slate quarries which nature has colonized with silver birches, by the much visited Bowder Stone (a fallen boulder of cubic shape), and out into the wider pasture around Rosthwaite, seen in the illustration. The main valley runs on to the tiny hamlet of Seatoller at the foot of the Honister Pass; a village which grew from an isolated farm to accommodate the workers at Honister Quarry at the top of the Pass. Further up the dale towards Seathwaite, on the fell-side to the north-west, the waste heaps of the once highly profitable plumbago mines can be seen. It was the discovery of this black lead that started pencil manufacture in Keswick, an industry which still exists but now uses imported lead.

109

Overhead line in the Seathwaite Valley, Dunnerdale. In the mid fifties the Electricity Board planned a major operation to supply 3,500 farms and 3,700 other rural premises that were still without a mains supply. The cost, it was estimated, would be about £2.5 million. If this task was to be carried out without great delay it was important that the sort of time-taking and expensive public inquiries held about the supply to Martindale, Langdale, and Borrowdale should be avoided. The Electricity Board divided its lakeland Area into 50 zones and special teams were formed to deal exclusively with rural electrification. A logical system of priorities was worked out so that progress was being made throughout the area, and the programme was rigidly maintained. Preliminary routes for the supply lines had to be worked out first, each zone being divided into a number of separate schemes. The Electricity Board then decided on consultation with the planners at this early stage and it was found possible to iron out some of the routing problems almost at the start; a consultation procedure which in this and other spheres has become a general practice. Sometimes the Planning Board decided that the National Park Commission should be consulted, and sometimes F.L.D. and other amenity bodies came into the negotiations. A mains electricity supply is now available for almost every property in the Lake District. Undergrounding and the careful routing of lines has meant that the countryside has not been put under a network of wires. On a journey into most dales by road or on a footpath little is to be seen of the supply lines.

110

The Duddon Valley road near Seathwaite, with overhead telephone lines. This length, erected in 1976, was soon afterwards realigned away from the road upon representations by F.L.D., and little is to be seen of telephone poles and wires in Dunnerdale today.

In the Lake District as a whole the routing of telephone lines and their replacement by aerial cable was for many years a matter of concern for the authorities and the amenity bodies. The operations of the Post Office Telephone Department were, and still are, virtually free from planning control. Up to the beginning of the 1960s an agreement had been made with the Regional Telephone Manager that there should be informal consultations on new lines with F.L.D. and in many cases the Department had willingly agreed to modifications to its proposals on suggestions made by the Society. After 1962 the consultation procedure was conducted directly with the Lake District Planning Board and F.L.D. representations went through this channel. One of the early cases that F.L.D. discussed with the Post Office was the Wasdale line which had run close to the shore of Wastwater. It was agreed to underground some sections of it and to re-route the line west of the road, well away from the lake. In recent times the whole line has been put underground.

Successful F.L.D. representations were also made for the removal of a line of poles over the lower slopes of Rannerdale Knotts above Crummock Water and for the undergrounding of aerial cable at High Cross between Hawkshead and Coniston where it marred the splendid view of the Coniston Fells. To the casual observer or to the speeding motorist telephone wires and poles in the countryside may seem matters of little consequence. But the accumulation of even small features, such as 'B&B' signs, and ranch-type fencing, can have a damaging impact on the countryside. Drawing attention to them, alone, has increased awareness of the delicate composition of the natural scene.

111

Wasdale on a cloudless February day with (left to right) Yewbarrow, Great Gable, and Lingmell. Scafell Pike and Scafell, England's highest mountains, adjoin Lingmell to the right. The scattered community of Wasdale Head, beyond the lake and beneath the slopes of Great Gable, remained without a mains supply of electricity until 1978. In the years between 1958 and 1965 the North West Electricity Board pursued an active policy of rural electrification and supplied many Lake District valleys with power. But the cost of a supply to Wasdale Head was so high and the return so small that the area was excluded from the scheme. Early in 1972 the residents of Wasdale Head again raised the question of a mains electricity supply and the Planning Board repeated to the Electricity Board its view that a supply line should be undergrounded along the whole length of Wasdale as the valley was one of the most unspoilt and isolated in the Lake District, that it was almost completely without tree cover, and entirely free from new development. It was not until 1977 that a solution was found when the cable was laid in the bed of Wastwater and underground beyond it, except for two short lengths which are adequately screened.

112

Laying the electricity cable in Wastwater. The Wasdale
electrification scheme was given a Civic Trust Award
in 1978.

*Illustration reproduced by kind permission of the copyright-
holder, North Western Electricity Board*

113

The tiny hamlet of Watendlath. This lies at the head of a narrow road which runs through a rocky and tortuous valley and which is a spur from the lower reaches of Borrowdale. The road is subject to much tourist pressure in summer-time. In the early seventies the then Cumberland County Council and the Countryside Commission carried out a detailed study of traffic problems and possible solutions. One scheme proposed was the type of experiment carried out in the Goyt Valley in Derbyshire involving the prohibition of non-essential vehicles from using the road at peak periods and the provision of alternative transport. The scheme entailed the establishment of a car park from which mini-buses would operate. A site in great Wood, the property of the National Trust, close to the beginning of the Watendlath road, was prepared. The plans came to nothing largely because of opposition from the local people who feared for one thing the loss of tourist trade. The National Trust went ahead with the car park in Great Wood, and in addition provided a hillside footpath link with other walking routes to Watendlath. The three and a half miles on foot to the hamlet, where pots of tea are plentiful, is a scenic and rewarding journey, well away from the frustrations of motoring on the road.

During the winter of 1978 Watendlath was provided with a mains electricity supply, the last hamlet in the Lake District to be connected. The necessity of undergrounding the cable in terrain of such 'high landscape value' was accepted without argument. The financial arrangements were similar to those worked out for Wasdale, in which the Electricity Board, the National Trust, the Countryside Commission, the Manpower Services Commission, and the Lake District Special Planning Board all played a part. There had been a great advance since the difficult and argumentative days over the Martindale and Borrowdale supplies.

The Windscale Nuclear Power Works from Seascale Hall. Built in the 1950s, they dominate the coastal scene with 400ft-high bulbous-topped chimneys and four cooling towers. Windscale is situated close to the shore, roughly half way between St Bees and Ravenglass; less than two miles south of the works is the attractive little Victorian resort of Seascale. The works are just outside the National Park boundary which reaches the coast at Drigg and runs along the shore to Silecroft. Windscale can be seen from many of the peaks, ridges, and slopes of the Lake District mountains, impinging on the westward view to a degree varying with distance, atmospheric conditions, and the extent of the steam plumes from the towers.

The *Cumbria Regional Planning Scheme* by Abercrombie and Kelly, prepared for the Cumberland County Council in 1932, set out the earliest suggested boundary for a 'national park area'. It included the coastal strip from Haverigg Point (west of Millom) to Seascale. In its first representations on the creation of National Parks, F.L.D. urged upon those Government Departments concerned during the war with this coast that it should be protected as an important part of a future National Park. Abercrombie and Kelly said that this narrow strip of land between the foot of the mountains and the sea was almost untouched by development and was worthy of the same standards of preservation as the mountainous area.

Eskmeals Gunnery Range is within this length of coastline, lying just south of the estuary of the River Esk. In 1948 and 1949 F.L.D. requested that use of this range and a number of other defence establishments in the Lake District should cease. The Service Departments eventually withdrew their claims on all sites except Eskmeals, about which however, certain agreements were reached concerning the places, times, and directions of firing. The Eskmeals Range is still operational and the noise of firing is at times to be heard along this coast and well inland.

Index

Numerals in italics refer to captions in Part Two

Abercrombie, Patrick, 4
Abraham Brothers, Keswick, 4, 21
Acts of Parliament
    Civic Amenities (1967), *81*
    Commons Registration (1965), *60*
    Countryside (1968), 4, 37, *66*
    Electricity (1919), 49
    Electricity (1947), 47
    Forestry (1919), 14
    Forestry (1951), 17
    Law of Property (1925), 60
    Manchester Corporation (1919), *9*
    Manchester Corporation Waterworks (1879),
        6, *65*
    Merchant Shipping (1894), *79*
    Motor Car (1903), 21
    National Parks and Access to the
        Countryside (1949), 4, 19, 35, *57, 62, 65*
    Planning (1947), *57*
    Town and Country Planning (1962), *73*
    Water (1973), 12
    Water Resources (1963), 12
    Wild Creatures and Wild Plants (1975), *83*
Afforestation, 14–17, *19–22, 58, 82*
Aira Force, *85*
Allerdale, District Council, 12
Ambleside, by-pass of, 33, *38*, 55
Anti-Noise League, 24
Armboth, *1*
Arnside, 30, *49*
Askham, *86*
Atomic Energy Commission, *99*

Bagot, Annette *and* Robin, 30
Barns, conversion of, *88*
Barrow-in-Furness, 30, *58*
Basinghall Mining Syndicate, 43
Bassenthwaite Lake, 29, 30, *8, 43, 44*
Berry, Geoffrey, 30
Birkett, Norman (later Lord), 15, 46, *8, 10, 26*
Birker Moor, 24, 25
Blencathra, 82
Boats, motor, 24, 37, 38, *66, 67, 77*
Bobbin-making, *20*
Borrowbeck Viaduct, *51, 52*
Borrowdale, *108*
Bowness Knott, *14*
Bowness-on-Windermere, *75*
Bowness Point, *21, 89*
Brandlehow Woods, *85*
Brathay, 40

British Leyland, 30, 31
British Nuclear Fuels, *13, 106, 114*
Brockhole, 40
Brotherikeld, *24*
Brothers Water, *66, 100*
Browncove Crags, *2*
Browning, Robert, *2*
Bursting Stones Quarry, *102, 103*
Buttermere, 15, 19, 23, 24
Buttermere Green Slate Company, 23, 47

Caldew, River, *92*
Calgarth, Seaplane factory, 37
Camping, 36, *73, 77*
Caravans, 36, *68, 69, 70, 73, 77*
Car Parking, 36, *36, 37, 40, 71, 72*
Castle Crag, *65, 68*
Castlerigg Stone Circle, *48*
Chorley, Lord, *26*
Cleave, Philip, *58*
Cocker, River, *3*
Cockermouth, *3*
Common land, *60*
Commons, Open Spaces and Footpaths
    Preservation Society, 4, 9
Coniston Old Man, *102, 103*
Coniston Water, 37, 38, *67, 76*
Copeland Borough Council, 12
Copper Mines Valley, *103*
Council for the Preservation of Rural England
    (C.P.R.E.), *9,* 11, 14–18, 25, 28, 29, *46, 82*
Countryside Commission, 12, 31, *49, 52, 63,*
    100
Crewdson, Robert, 7
Crossley, Herbert, 22
Crossman, Richard, *11*
Crummock Water, *3*, 15
Cumberland
    Countryside Conference, 37
    County Council, 22, 29
    Development Council, 31
    population of, 21
Cumbria
    County Council, 12
    rivers of, *11*
Cumbria Naturalists' Trust, 17, *84*
Cumbria Tourist Board, *75*
Cumbrian Regional Planning Scheme, 24, *114*

Derwent River, *8*
Derwent Water, 38, 44, *59, 82, 108*

Dower, John
    afforestation negotiations by, 15
    Report on National Parks by, 4, 19, 28, 47,
        82
Drainage schemes, 17
Drigg Ordnance Factory, 106
Duddon valley, 16, 17, 22, 24, 48, 110
    Bridge, 24
Dunmail Raise, 1, 25, 31, 35, 96
Dunnerdale, 15

Eaton, Arthur, 31
Ehen, River, 14
Electrification
    Industrial, 44, 46, 52
    rural, 46–49, 51, 53, 58, 108, 109, 111, 112,
        113
Elterwater, 101
English Lake District Association, 2, 3
Ennerdale, 8, 10, 11, 12, 13, 14, 15, 19, 21, 23,
    40, 89, 98
Environment, Department of the, 29
Erosion, 64
Eskdale, 14–17, 24, 48, 58
Eskmeals Gunnery Range, 114

Farm buildings, 93
Farming, 5, 16–18, 24–26, 36, 63, 85, 94, 96–98
Finsthwaite Heights, 20, 71
Fishing, 67
Flood prevention, 17
Footpaths, 3, 31, 39, 41, 43, 61, 63–65, 89
Forest
    parks, 14, 16
    trails, 40, 89
Forestry Commission, 2, 14, 16, 18, 19, 21, 23,
    24, 27, 40
Freshwater Biological Association, 40
Friars Crag, 108
Friends of the Lake District (F.L.D.), 4, 58, 60,
    65
    Campaigns of,
        Electrification, 46, 58, 108, 109, 111, 113
        Forestry, 14–17, 19, 23–24, 29, 58
        Mining, 92, 107
        Roads, 22, 24, 25, 27, 30, 32, 33, 39, 53
            (A66), 28, 31, 32, 45, 56
        Telephone lines, 110
        Traffic, 80
        Water, 3, 8, 9, 11

Gatesgarth Pass, 12, 23, 53
Glencoyne Bay, 71–72
Glenridding, 10, 83, 99
Great Gable, 57, 106
Great Langdale, 17, 60, 61
Greenside Lead Mine, 43, 45, 99
Greta, Bridge, 42, 46, 48
    River, 29, 41
Gunpowder mills, 13, 42

Hardknott
    Forest Park, 14, 16

    Pass, 22, 24, 25, 32, 75
Harter Fell, 6, 24
Hartsop, 26, 63, 66, 100
Hause Gill, 23, 24
Haweswater
    public access, 6
    water abstraction, 4, 5, 9, 39
Hawkshead, 80
Haythornthwaite, Gerald, 45
Helvellyn, 2, 41, 47, 64, 83
Herdwick Sheep, 96
Hervey, Canon G. A. K., 84
Hill, Octavia, 4, 7
Hobhouse Committee, 19, 47
Holford-Walker, Alan F., 29
Holiday cottages, 90, 98
Honister Hause, 22–24
    Pass 21
    Slate at, 2, 42, 108
House conversions, 88
Howtown, 30
Hydro-electric schemes, 48, 58

Innominate Tarn, 57
Iron ore, 2

Kelly, Sydney, 25
Kendal, bypass of, 33, 56
Keswick, bypass of, 29, 30, 32, 33, 46
Kirkstone Pass, 25, 26, 40
    Quarry, 44, 104

Lake District
    afforestation, 14, 19, 20
    birdlife, 40, 84
    boating, 66
    car-parking, 36, 71
    fishing, 67
    house-ownership, 41, 88, 90–91, 98
    industries, 13
    litter, 81
    motoring in, 21, 24, 26, 32
    noise, 24
    population, 21, 98
    recreation in, 61, 100
    traffic censuses, 26–27
    traffic management, 40
    tourists, 2, 23, 41, 68, 72, 75
    unemployment, 19, 20
    walking in, 24, 40–41
    woodlands, 19
Lake District Advertising Association, 3
Lake District Defence Association, 7
Lake District Defence Society, 2
Lake District Farm Estates, 16, 26
Lake District Planning Board, 4, 19, 27, 29, 31,
    53
    development control by, 86, 92–93
    Information services of, 40–41
    National Park Plan, 70
    Upland Management Service, 63
Lake District Safeguarding Society, 3
Lake District Ski Club, 39, 83

Lake District Tourist Board, *59*
Langdale Pikes, *60, 85*
Larch trees, 13, 15, 18–19
Latrigg, protest marches to, 3, 33, *45*
Lead mines, 42–43
Levens Bridge, *16*, 30
    Park, *54*
Limefitt Caravan Site, *68*
Limestone pavements, 45, *105*
    quarries, *45*
Lindale, *50*
Litter, *81*
Liza, River, 22
Longsleddale, 7, 11, *12*, 53
Lonsdale, Earl of, *85*
Loweswater, 15, 18

M6 *see* Roads
Manchester water abstraction by, *1–2, 4–6, 10,*
    31, 53
Manesty Woods, *59, 85*
Mardale, flooded village of, *4, 5, 7, 9, 11*
Martindale, *30*
Mining, 42, *92*
Morecambe Bay, water schemes, 9
Mosedale, *92*
Motor boats, 24, 37, 38, *66*
    cars, 21, 26, 27, 32, 34
'Mountain Goat' mini-'buses, *34*

National Parks, early years, 3, 4, 35, 54, 59, *94,*
    98
    Dower Report on, 4, 19, *81, 82, 86, 97*
    Hobhouse Committee, (1947), 19, *57*
    Planning controls, 28, *70*
    Sandford Committee (1974), 4, *61*
    Voluntary Wardens *81, 97*
National Trust, foundation of, 4
    policies, 11, 15, 16, *24, 27, 37, 71, 85, 89, 100*
National Water Council, 10
Nature Conservancy Council, *84, 100*
Nature Reserves, *84*
Nature Trails, *31*, 40
Newby Bridge, *16*
Newlands Pass, 24
Noise, 24, 38, *76*
North West Electricity Board, 47, 49, 52, *109,*
    111, 113
North West Study Group on Traffic, 28
North West Water Authority, 2, *9*, 10, 11, *13,*
    89

Patterdale, *63*
Pencil making, 42
Pillar Mountain, *21–23*
Pollution, 107
Public Inquiries
    camping, *73*
    caravan sites, *68, 73*
    electricity, *30, 44, 49*, 51
    lake speed restrictions, *79*
    roads, 30, *41, 54, 55*
    water, 3, *10, 13*

Quarrying, 44, 45, *101, 102*

Railways
    Braithwaite and Buttermere, 2
    Kendal to Windermere, 1, 2, 21
    Lancaster to Carlisle, *12*
    London to Glasgow, *51*
    Windermere to Ambleside, 3
        freight carrying, 2, 44
        tourist traffic, 2
        Wordsworth's views on, 2
Raise, *83*
Ramblers' Association, 28, 31, 39, *82*
Rannerdale Knotts, 3
Rawnsley, Canon H. D., 3, 4, 6, 7
    Eleanor, 3
Rippon, Geoffrey, 31, 32
Roads
    early systems, 21
    heavy traffic on, 27, *38, 39, 46, 52*
    toll, 23
    width of, 24–26
    A6, 25, 28, 29–32, *49, 52*
    A66, *41–44, 46, 47, 82*
    A590, *16, 49, 50*
    A591, 2, 25, 26, 33, 34, 35, *37–39, 44, 56*
    A592, 25, *40, 73*
    A594, 28, 29
    A595, 24, 25, 30, *33*
    A685, *52*
    B5305, 30
    M6, 27, 29, 30, 33, 41, *51–54*
Rothay Hotel, *95*
Ruskin, John, 2, 7
Rusland Beeches, *29*
Rydal Water, 37

Sailing, 31, *76, 77*
St. John's Vale, 25, *41*
Sandford Committee on National Park Policies
    (1974), 4, *61*
Satterthwaite, *20, 88*
Scafell, *58, 62, 74*
Scalehill Bridge, 3
Schon, Sir Frank (later Lord), 31
Scott, Francis C., *26*, 40
Seascale, *114*
Seatoller, 23
Sebergham, 32, *41*
Sheep-farming, 2, 14, 16, *94, 96*
Sitka spruce, 14
Skating, *59*
Skiddaw, *8*
Skiing, snow, 39, *83, 99*
    water, 37, *76*
Slate, 2, 23, 42–44, 53, *67, 101–104*
Somervell, Sir Arthur, 15
    Robert, 7
Spence, Kenneth, 4
Staveley, bypass of, 34, *56*
Stokes, Lord, 32
Stott Park Bobbin Mill, *20*
Swindale, 9, *9*

Symonds, Rev. H. H., 4, 15, 20, 22–23, 26, 53, 65

Telephone lines, *110*
Thirlmere, afforestation, 14
  nature trails, *31*
  water abstraction, *1, 5, 6, 8, 10*
Thirlspot, *1*
Thornthwaite, 14
Tourism, 20, 23, 41, *68, 72, 75, 88, 95*
Traffic, *34, 80, 113*
  censuses, 26, 27, 33
  North-West Study Group, 28
Transport, Ministry of, 22, 24, 25, 29
Tree felling in wartime, 18
Tree planting, 16, *27, 28, 71, 73, 100*
Trees
  beech, *29*
  larch, 13, 15, 18, 19
  Norway spruce, 14, *22*
  oak, *2*, 15, 18, *54*
  Scots pine, 13
  Sitka spruce, 14, 15

Ullock Pike, 8
Ullswater
  pollution of, *107*
  speed restrictions, 38, *76*
  water abstraction, 4, 10, *10*
Ulpha, 23
Upland Management Service, 41, *63*

Wabberthwaite, 24
Walking, 19, *21, 22, 24, 32, 53, 61, 64, 65, 74, 89, 99*
Walpole, Hugh, 14

Wartime restrictions, *30, 106, 114*
Wasdale, 52, *62, 111*
Wastwater, 8, *106, 110*
Watendlath, 2, 52, *112–113*
Water abstraction from
  Bassenthwaite Lake, *8*
  Crummock Water, *3*, 8
  Duddon valley, *58*
  Ennerdale Water, 8, *13, 14, 21*
  Haweswater, 5, 9, 10, *10*
  Morecambe Bay, 9, 10, 31
  River Derwent, 12
  Thirlmere, *1, 5, 6, 8, 10*
  Ullswater, *4, 6*, 10, 11, *87*
  Wastwater, 8
  Windermere, 11, *14*, 21, *87*
Water Resources Board, 9, *11*
Westmorland County Council, 25
Westmorland population, 21
Wet Sleddale, *4*, 9, *18, 19*
Whinlatter Pass, 24, *24*
Whitbarrow, *84*
Whitehaven, 8, 10, 11, *13*
Whiteless Pike, *3*
White Moss Common, *37*
Wilson, Rt. Hon. Harold, M.P., 32
  Hugh, 30, *40*
Windermere, *16, 79, 87, 91*
Windscale, *13*, 52, *114*
Winster Valley, *11*
Womersley, J. Lewis, 30, *40*
Wordsworth, William, 2, 7, *13, 37*
Wrynose Pass, 22, 24, *32, 34, 75*
Wythburn, 1, 2

Youth Hostels, *12, 99, 103*